T0270038

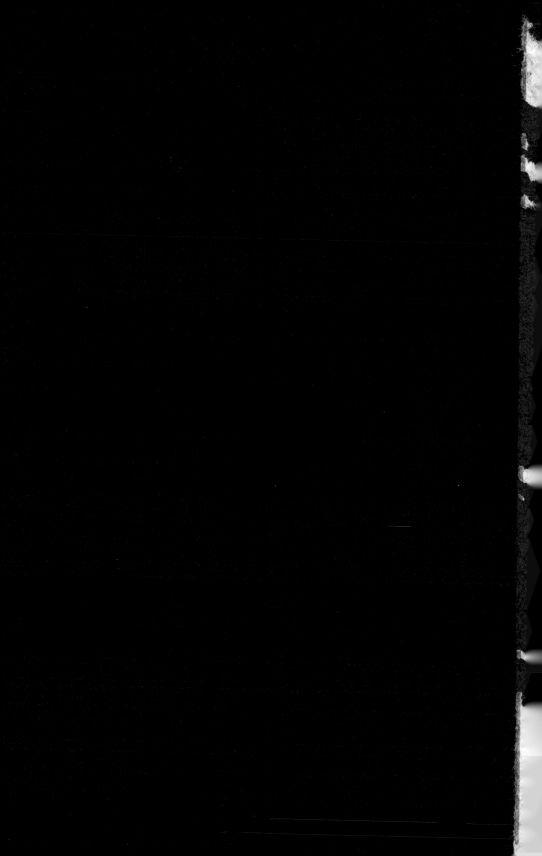

Praise for deComplify

"Gary Michel's book, *deComplify: How Simplification Drives Stability, Innovation, and Transformation*, is a game-changer for anyone seeking to navigate today's complex business landscape. With practical insights and actionable strategies, Michel empowers leaders to cut through the noise, streamline processes, and unlock new levels of success. This book is a must-read guide for those looking to deliver breakthrough performance and transform their organizations for the better."

—**Stan Askren,** former CEO and chairman, HNI Corporation

"*deComplify* is a must-read for anyone seeking to navigate the complexities of our world with renewed clarity, purpose, and simplicity. This book is a beacon, providing a roadmap to simplify complex situations and uncover hidden opportunities. The author's ability to break down intricate concepts into actionable steps is truly remarkable. Through relatable examples and thought-provoking anecdotes, *deComplify* will equip you with the tools, mindset, and inspiration to simplify your life, fuel innovation, and create lasting change. Prepare to be inspired, enlightened, and transformed by this groundbreaking book. Get ready to unlock your full potential and unleash the power of simplicity."

—**Damon Baker,** CEO, Lean Focus

"Michel provides a practical road map in *deComplify,* based on his successful application of the four leadership absolutes employed throughout his career. A great read to understand how to reduce complexity and deliver results."

—**John Holland,** former CEO and chairman, Butler Manufacturing

"In *deComplify*, Gary Michel has both identified and solved one of the most common yet least understood challenges in business today—the tendency to overcomplicate or 'complify' business challenges and processes. Michel provides a much-needed road map to personal and organizational effectiveness. This book should be required reading for all leaders and aspiring leaders in business today."

—**William L. Sparks,** Ph.D., Author of Amazon #1 best-selling book,
*Actualized Leadership: Meeting Your Shadow & Maximizing Your
Potential;* Distinguished chair and professor of leadership,
McColl School of Business, Queens University of Charlotte

"Gary Michel has captured business wisdom in a framework that can simplify the most complex business challenges! Deeply engaging and starkly relevant, *deComplify* will inspire you to lead from a position of insatiable learning."

—**Katy Dickson,** former president, American Girl; Board director,
Flexsteel Industries, Black Rifle Coffee, and Compana Pet

"For those who wish to remain stuck in theoretical constructs and impractical suggestions, *deComplify* is not the book for you. But if you crave a firsthand perspective from a proven business mastermind and operator, this book is a gold mine. Filled with dynamic strategies on employing lean design and engaged leadership, *deComplify* is your roadmap to business advancement, offering a pioneering approach to achieving stability, sparking innovation, and leading transformative change."

—**John Rossman,** Business advisor; Best-selling author,
*The Amazon Way, The Amazon Way on IoT,
Think Like Amazon;* Keynote speaker

"Gary's approach to business draws upon a wealth of practical experience and is both actionable and personable, highly recommended."

—**Mark Morelli,** CEO, Vontier Corporation

"In *deComplify*, Gary Michel shares a crucial message about how effective leaders engage and motivate team members with clear, direct communications that sets expectations and drives business outcomes. This is an area where Michel excels as a leader, and I am grateful for his valuable insights in this important book."

—**Dean Acosta,** Former Honeywell & Resideo Chief communications officer.

"*deComplify* is a great example of Gary Michel's ability to present important thoughts in ways that everyone can relate to. Knowing him for many years personally and wotking together on several boards I have come to truly respect Gary's leadership qualities. While much of Gary's experience is in the manufacturing world, the concepts in deComplify have application in a wide range of industries."

—**Barry Bobrow,** Managing director, Regions Bank

As someone who has benefited directly from Gary's wisdom and experience, I can attest to the value created by continuously working to "deComplify". Gary is able to incorporate and apply his concepts across the enterprise, from the shop floor to long-term strategic planning. Most importantly, Gary "deComplifies" the presentation of his message by providing advice that is easy to understand and execute. Well done!

—**Brad Hughes,** retired CEO, Cooper Tire & Rubber Company

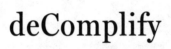

deComplify

deComplify

v. | *How Simplicity Drives*
Stability, Innovation,
and Transformation

Gary S. Michel

Forbes | Books

Published by Forbes Books, Charleston, South Carolina.
Member of Advantage Media.

Forbes Books is a registered trademark, and the Forbes Books colophon is a trademark of Forbes Media, LLC.

Printed in the United States of America.

10 9 8 7 6 5 4 3 2 1

ISBN: 979-8-88750-341-7 (Hardcover)
ISBN: 979-8-88750-342-4 (eBook)

Library of Congress Control Number: 2023908760

Cover and layout design by Lance Buckley.

This custom publication is intended to provide accurate information and the opinions of the author in regard to the subject matter covered. It is sold with the understanding that the publisher, Forbes Books, is not engaged in rendering legal, financial, or professional services of any kind. If legal advice or other expert assistance is required, the reader is advised to seek the services of a competent professional.

Since 1917, Forbes has remained steadfast in its mission to serve as the defining voice of entrepreneurial capitalism. Forbes Books, launched in 2016 through a partnership with Advantage Media, furthers that aim by helping business and thought leaders bring their stories, passion, and knowledge to the forefront in custom books. Opinions expressed by Forbes Books authors are their own. To be considered for publication, please visit **books.Forbes.com**.

To Jodi, with love.

You have always been in my corner,
had my back, and walked by my side.

This is the Way for those who want to learn my strategy:

Do not think dishonestly.

The Way is in the training.

Become acquainted with every art.

Know the Ways of all professions.

Distinguish between gain and loss in worldly matters.

Develop intuitive judgement and understanding of everything.

Perceive those things which cannot be seen.

Pay attention even to trifles.

Do nothing which is of no use.

—MIYAMOTO MUSASHI, *A BOOK OF FIVE RINGS*

Contents

Introduction

*Life is really simple, but we insist
on making it complicated.*

—CONFUCIUS

Complify. It's a word. It means to make something more complicated than it needs to be. As a young leader early in one of my first leadership roles, I was frustrated with the many layers of processes put in place to solve a problem. These so-called solutions only obscured the root issue and led to more complications.

A colleague shared this same frustration and uttered, "I wish they wouldn't complify things so much!" This word stuck with me for decades.

Through a series of leadership roles in various segments and industries, I returned again and again to complify to express my frustration with the tendency of executives and managers to respond to the existing complexities of business by making things even more complicated. I have used the term so prolifically that it has become a sort of trademark for my leadership style.

Over my career, I have had the opportunity to work in a number of businesses in different industries and markets with different business models. I have found several similarities in each and every business. It boils down to this: Successful businesses share essentially the same strategy. Every successful business seeks to outgrow the competition and continuously improve the business to expand profitability. It's that simple.

You'd be forgiven for thinking that businesspeople actually love complexity. No sooner is a simple business successful than its managers seem to pour energy into making it much more complicated. The truth is that people tend to unintentionally complify matters when they attempt to solve problems. Faced with existing complexities in an organization, the standard response is to *cope* with the symptoms rather than isolate and reduce the source of the problem.

To react in the moment is to fail to recognize that an organizational structure has evolved over time in a way that no longer makes sense in the present or for the future. Additionally, unquestioningly accepting the number of products and services the business offers only complifies the portfolio. A decomplified approach helps recognize when product offerings have proliferated beyond what's practical to produce or desirable to the customer. Meanwhile, operational processes get tweaked and augmented in order to make short-term fixes, only to produce longer-term problems. In so many ways, when leadership takes their eyes off the ball, complification increases.

This distracting and complifying mindset comes at a huge cost, in both financial and emotional terms. Fundamentally, the stacking effect of complification becomes an ever-increasing barrier to transforming a business into a great company. Decomplifying is more than the stripping away of excess. Real decomplifying streamlines processes *for a purpose*. That purpose is to create a great company.

A great company is a company that people want to buy from, people want to work for, and people want to invest in. A truly great company always does the right thing for people, communities, and the world itself. This definition of a great company embodies the fundamental elements of a successful organization implicitly. It calls out the importance of the customer relationship and the need to provide differentiated and superior value through products and services. It recognizes the importance of engaged associates who not only create and deliver the value of the enterprise but also derive benefits themselves. And, as you would expect, a great company must make attractive returns for its investors through growth, operational excellence, and sustainable productivity.

A great company is one that people want to buy from, people want to work for, and people want to invest in. A truly great company always does the right thing for people, communities, and the world itself.

People want to buy from a great company because they like the products and services, find it easy to do business with it, and see value in the relationship. People want to work for a great company because they believe in the purpose and values of the company and feel they can contribute and realize their personal and career aspirations. People want to invest in a great company because it continuously delivers superior financial returns.

These essential relationships apply to almost every business, regardless of product or service, industry, or geography. In this book, some but not all examples focus on manufacturing, but any kind of work can benefit from a decomplified approach. At the heart of decomplification, is the desire to eliminate artificial barriers to value delivery, which scales from the smallest unit of work to running an entire enterprise.

Jumping off the definition of a great company as one that people want to buy from, work with, and invest in, what can leaders do to make their companies great? John Rossman[1] wrote eloquently about the Amazon Way's fourteen leadership principles that contributed to making Amazon a great company. Boiling that down to what fits all business models and organizations, I swear by four leadership absolutes. The Decomplified Absolutes are:

1. *Obsess about Customers*
2. *Field the Right Team*
3. *Own Your Dependencies*
4. *Deliver Results*

How you practice the Decomplified Absolutes is visible in your leadership, culture, values, customer experience, employee engagement, and investor relations. As you navigate these core functions of your business, processes need to be simple, clean, and uncomplicated. If your business core is burdened with unnecessary work and delays, then you need to focus on the absolutes to eliminate the nonessentials. Decomplifying leads to clarifying the workflows and operational activities for customers, employees, leaders, and investors. Then, by staying true to the Decomplified Absolutes progress toward greatness is unimpeded.

Great companies figure out how to continuously outgrow the competition, sustainably expand earnings over time, and through many business cycles and deliver a greater purpose that customers, associates, and investors value. Through innovation, product management, and segmentation, they consistently deliver solutions that their customers desire. By embracing the practice of decomplification, you can transform your business into a great company and make sure you keep it that way. Of course, most businesses are complex. They consist

---

1   John Rossman, *The Amazon Way: Amazon's 14 Leadership Principles* (Clyde Hill Publishing, 2014).

of multiple forces that constantly change in the way they interact with each other. That makes simplification very challenging. But a complex business can decomplify their processes and operations, and returns will soar.

Simple, Complex, and Complicated

Simplicity lives in business models that are *reliably boring and relentlessly repeatable*. Simplicity is not aspirational because it's exciting. Simplicity is not running to a fire; it's enjoying the freedom to grow your business or invest in your employees because there's no fire to fight. Simplicity is the deadbolt on your front door that lets you get the good night's sleep that energizes you to accomplish your dreams.

Repeatability follows simplicity. If your processes can be self-sustaining and withstand the need for tinkering, then you can watch the market to take advantage of opportunities instead of constantly catching up with fluctuations because your processes are not stable. This is what Jim Collins called *The Flywheel Effect*.[2] Once you build a solid, repeatable process, you let it do its thing while you tinker with the art of the possible and develop strategy. Throwing junk on the flywheel is inadvisable—that's just complifying things.

Now, simplification and repeatability require work. To get there, you need to decomplify what is in your way and, just as importantly, prevent stakeholders, employees, and yourself from decomplifying things in new ways.

Decomplification is the antidote to complexity. Let's start with the difference between the words *complicated* and *complex*. They are

---

2   Jim Collins, "Jim Collins-Concepts-The Flywheel Effect," Jim Collins, 2022, https://www.jimcollins.com/concepts/the-flywheel.html.

similar but not the same, and understanding the difference is key to avoiding the former and addressing the latter. We can address this dichotomy between complex and complicated by *navigating the complex* and *eliminating the complicated.*

Complexity is the nature of intricate and layered systems. There is no verb tense for complex. It is a state of being. Things can be complex due to their nature. It is difficult, but not impossible, to understand complex systems. We can reduce complexity in some processes, but many efficiencies that make things work better are, themselves, inherently complex. Quantum computing, for example, is not going to become less complex as it gets more efficient. Complexity is not frightening or bad; it's simply a challenge everyone faces in different facets of work.

Complicated, on the other hand, is a noun and has a verb tense. It's also an artificial state created by actions or circumstances that can be addressed. Humans excel at complicating things. When they complicate the complex systems, people create mazes for the other people who are trying to map them, which is a direct affront to the four Decomplified Absolutes.

Process Debt and Recovery

Technical debt is a term common to software development and coding. Essentially, when software engineers intentionally fail to fix known issues to make a deadline, they are incurring technical debt. Over time, this list of inefficiencies grows and makes for low-quality and unstable software products. However, this concept of technical debt is relevant to *any* work that humans do. I call the larger concept *process debt* because it occurs when we knowingly refuse to correct an error or inefficiency in the interest of maintaining the status quo.

> *Process debt is the accumulation of inefficiencies, bottlenecks, and other issues that arise as a result of neglecting to improve or update a process. It typically results from choosing short-term results over long-term solutions.*

Regardless of the domain, be it manufacturing, finance, customer service, sales, etc., every short cut taken and every extra person thrown at a problem that can't be solved outright is an action that drives process debt. Likewise, every time the *easy* thing is decided and done instead of the right thing, in the interest of perceived time savings, more process debt is created.

Decomplifying drives recovery and prevention of process debt by changing the behaviors that lead to creating process debt in the first place. When striving to decomplify processes and approaches, one can identify existing process debts and can then successfully eliminate them. One key methodology for helping us decomplify and eliminate process debt is Lean.

Leaning into Lean

The Lean business system is an offshoot from manufacturing but is entirely extensible to all layers of business projects and operations. Lean is key to avoiding and paying down process debt because the purpose of Lean is to eliminate waste in everything we do. We can banish complifying activities that hamper innovation or productivity, such as time wasted in non-value-added meetings and activities or adhering to needlessly convoluted protocols. Eliminating waste cuts costs, reduces the time taken to deliver products and services to customers, and even makes it easier to arrive at effective strategic decisions and deploy innovative solutions. Eliminating waste is at the heart of Lean systems thinking.

In practice, Lean is a methodology that has existed for more than seventy years, and leaders still struggle with implementing it. Lean is all about simplicity. It really comes down to maximizing customer value while minimizing waste in the production process. This is achieved by reducing the time it takes to complete a process (cycle time) and increasing the time spent on value-adding activities

Lean is key to avoiding and paying down process debt because the purpose of Lean is to eliminate waste in everything we do.

(process cycle efficiency). Improving this relationship eliminates waste and frees up capacity for growth. This is equally true in factory operations as it is across larger business practices. It is entirely scalable. Lean is simple, but it is not easy.

Lean is a great tool for decomplified organizations. Decomplified organizations work in a simple manner and operate with a degree of calmness and refined organization. They remove much of the complexity that inhibits performance. One of my early lean sensei (coach) described it as a symphony—when everything is operating properly, you can hear beautiful music. But if just one instrument misses a note, the result is displeasing. Achieving this level of simplicity, however, is not easy.

A strong Lean approach provides the tools required to operate effectively and efficiently, employing the very essence of lean, the practice of continuous improvement, respect for people, identification and elimination of waste, problem identification, and problem-solving. Fundamentally, organizations are in a state of simplicity when their day-to-day activities are properly aligned with exactly what the business needs to do to drive performance, also known as strategy.

At the very core of the Lean approach is the development and deployment of standard work. We define standard work as the *best known way*. This is important. It is premature and inaccurate to document and measure ourselves against a theoretical or aspirational level of performance.

Rather, focus on understanding how to best perform the process to achieve the desired outcome. Then, look to continuously improve the process by eliminating waste and deploying *new best known ways* to perform the work. Each of us needs to feel empowered to improve the processes that we touch every day to establish a problem-solving culture. The people who do the work are creating value, and they best understand the work that they do. Empowering them to do their work more effectively is the fastest way to improve quality and drive employee satisfaction and a positive culture.

Every associate must be a problem solver. Organizations should not rely on leaders to provide all the answers. When leaders coach others to become problem-solvers, they free up their own capacity to take on proactive thinking and tasks, increasing the company's ability to improve, change and grow. This approach helps develop associates and future leaders. It provides opportunities for growth and enhances engagement.

Reinforcing the basics of standard work, problem identification and problem solving, and management by daily improvement is imperative to transforming operations and functional processes to the next level. In other words, we talk about the transformation standard as *halving the bad and doubling the good*.

This simplicity forces us to identify the most important area of focus at a given time for improvement and helps to eliminate confusion and frustration that is sometimes experienced when processes are not optimized. The simplicity that comes with the successful deployment of a Lean business operating system is a way of life. It becomes part of the continuous improvement culture and dedication to serving customers with a differentiated and superior experience. This experience drives growth and gives us vision for even more opportunities for improvement and innovation.

Activity is aligned with strategy. Again, it's that simple. When this alignment occurs, you create more bandwidth for business-critical tasks that accelerate performance.

The business cost of complification is huge in both financial and emotional terms. Complification distracts your focus away from making dramatic breakthroughs while achieving continuous improvement—a combination that is necessary for a company to thrive and grow.

Clarity is key. In seeking to decomplify, distill thoughts and communication to the essential. This streamlining keeps inferences and guesswork to a minimum. In explaining the wild success of Amazon, John Rossman writes in The Amazon Way[3], "Amazon's leaders work hard to make their thinking very clear—to be clear not only about what they decide but also precisely why they decide as they do." When your own thinking is clear, you can understand and articulate your choices. If the thinking is unclear, there is a greater likelihood of complifying a situation.

Setting Things in Motion

In the spirit of helping you decomplify your business, I offer clear advice that is easy to understand and illustrated with some real-life and instructive examples. I am an engineer at heart, and I like realistic, practical solutions to everyday problems. I'm interested in practices and

---

3   Rossman, *The Amazon Way*, xxvi.

strategies that deliver reliably boring, relentlessly repeatable outcomes, despite all the unavoidable complexities and unknown factors. Those solutions are what I believe lead to outsized business performance.

In the following chapters, we will look at how you can decomplify your business to deliver breakthrough performance that will excite customers, engage associates, and attract investors. We will examine how decomplification will help you achieve and sustain the definition of a great company: one that people want to buy from, people want to work for, and investors want to invest in. By applying a decomplified approach, you can develop the skills and focus to make a real impact on your own life, your family, your friends, your community, and your business.

Because leadership impacts the rest of an organization, we begin with what decomplified leadership looks like and how we can achieve it.

1.   *Go and See*

Farming looks mighty easy when your plow is a pencil,
and you're a thousand miles from the corn field.

—DWIGHT D. EISENHOWER

As a leader, it is your responsibility to ensure that your culture is healthy enough to raise, clarify, and align expectations, remove barriers that hinder execution of your strategy, and motivate your teams to perform. Leaders decomplify by reducing waste and increasing efficiency in their own decision-making processes before they attempt to do the same with the company, products, or people. We set aside impulse and ego to get to the heart of leadership.

Decomplifying works faster and better when everyone in an organization knows exactly why they are there and what they are there to do. A rallying cry is a great way to align understanding and stimulate motivation in an organization. One of the best examples I've seen of a successful rallying cry comes from the organization Samaritan's Feet. Their rallying cry is front and center, and it's not complicated: "Samaritan's Feet provides shoes to those in need around the world." The organization, founded by Manny Ohonme, is a passion project. Manny won his first pair of shoes at the age of nine in a basketball contest. Manny knew, instinctively and with his whole heart, that everyone deserves shoes, and they should be a human right, not a prize to be won. Shoes are a need, and Manny found a way to meet that need.

This captures what they do, "deliver shoes to people," and why they do it, "the people are in need." The rallying cry doesn't get into the details about the great need for those shoes, the logistical concerns about getting and distributing the shoes, or the extraordinary impact a good pair of shoes has for the nine and a half million people they have helped. The rallying cry will also help them stay focused on their most immediate goal, which they can also effectively share with donors and stakeholders. This means that they have brought shoes to nine million people, and their present goal is to drive that number to ten million. Simple, direct, and attainable—all in their rallying cry. Those are the causes, processes, and effects of their work, but the rallying cry is more simple—provide shoes to those in need.

> *A rallying cry is a unifying and motivating call to action used to inspire and align a team toward a common objective.*

A rallying cry is a unifying and motivating call to action used to inspire and align a team toward a common objective.

Keeping the rallying cry simple enables everyone, including and especially leadership, to ask, "Is the work I do every day adding to the reason I am here? Does the process I see in front of me help or hinder my ability to serve the rallying cry?"

It's so easy to get lost in the weeds of the work, and a rallying cry serves as a reality check to ensure we are all heading in the same direction and gives us confidence to correct course at the individual and organizational level when we find ourselves complifying our work.

The best leaders not only share a rally cry, but they also live by it, and they ensure that their associates can live by it as well. They remove barriers or obstacles when their people cannot deliver on the promise of their purpose at work. Great leaders are not afraid of seeing, owning, and ultimately fixing errors to correct course and lead in the right direction. Providing a rallying cry and living by it provides the organization and its people a focal point and the motivation to deliver on the promise and the purpose of the work. All of this is transformative for a healthier culture and an engaged and productive workforce.

Decomplifying your leadership style requires modeling the behaviors that will decomplify your organization. In *A Book of Five Rings*, Miyamato instructs, "If you wish to lead others, you must first know yourself,"[4] and that wisdom still stands. So, begin with your own standard work. Assess yourself, discover what you do every day, week, month, and quarter, and determine whether or not the things you are doing and the way you invest your time are decomplifying or complifying your life and, subsequently, your leadership. Then ruthlessly eliminate tasks and activities that do not add value. If tasks add value but are in the way of higher-value activities, delegate the lower-value tasks. Decomplifying starts with you and how easy you make it for everyone else to decomplify your business.

I recently went on a Gemba walk at a factory in Florida. Gemba walks are a tool from Lean methodology where leaders go to the place where the work is done and value is added. We did what is called a stand-in-a-circle exercise, where we do just that, stand in a fixed location on the factory floor to simply observe the work. This is where I met Max.

Max was on the glazing line and was placing glass in window frames. Max's work is essential. When Max does it right, the company

---

4   Miyamoto Musashi, *A Book of Five Rings*, trans. Victor Harris (The Overlook Press, 1974).

makes quality products and has satisfied paying customers. If Max does his job poorly, even once, the costs can be significant. A great company does not fail to deliver the right product to the customer on time. Introducing obstacles to that basic premise sabotages success. Delays and dissatisfied customers are all long-term problems that flow from a short-term misstep.

It's essential that Max can do a good job and focus on placing the glass in the frame to the best of his ability. This is Max's standard work. So, we watched Max, and he was running about 100 steps back and forth between jobs just to find the correct sheet of glass to fit into the window frame. This pattern repeated over and over, and it was not meant to be in Max's standard work, but he was adapting to the environment to honor his responsibilities. The repeated journeys away from his station added no value to Max, the customer, the workers down the line, or the company. In fact, all this movement and disruption caused cycle time issues and introduced the opportunity for defects.

When we debriefed with Max and brought up the repeated trips away from his work area to retrieve glass, he explained that he did check the cart closest to him, but more often than not, the correct glass was not in close proximity to him, so he had to go find the right one. This is more problematic than just having the cart too far away and needing to walk to it. No, Max had to visit multiple carts to find the exact glass he needed to complete a window. I like to think of Max and others doing skilled assembly work, like a surgeon. The product he is making is his patient. Just like we would not expect the surgeon to leave the patient alone on the table to go find a particular scalpel, Max should not leave the window line. To prevent waste, Max should have everything he needs within reach, or someone, like the surgical nurse does for the doctor, would be there to provide what he needs when he needs it. Instead, Max was losing time and creating anxiety by seeking the correct parts and then bringing them back to his workspace.

The root of Max's problem turned out to be the company's supply chain struggles. Because of glass shortages, window production was not running in sequenced order. So, Max had to hunt around to find the right glass for the window he was trying to build. This meant he had to search around for the glass on the correct cart, with the right glass, for the right window, and improvise (or adjust) the sequence of windows he could complete. This was impacting the ability to complete full orders for customers. Max was improvising and getting work done, which was admirable, but the work he was getting done was not aligned with business commitments to deliver products based on order cycle time.

Max was never the problem. Max was doing his best to be productive, and he was finishing the work he was able to do. The process was the problem. However, without Max, we would not have understood the root of our problem. Watching Max step away from his work and lose time seeking something he should have had at hand was a clear indictment of our processes and a direct result of supply issues outside of Max's control. Additionally, we were able to target some solutions because we could see and address the gaps between Max's standard work, the process debt (leaving his station repeatedly to find the right glass), and the reason for the deviation in Max's cycle time.

---

*The people doing the work are in the best
position to improve that work.*

Max had a great attitude and was happy to do his work and deal with the challenges of parts in unknown places. He didn't just stop, like a machine might, if the wrong part came his way. Rather, he sought it out. He was solving the problem within his proximity. Max could also tell us what we could do to make his job easier and lead to better customer satisfaction.

The people doing the work are in the best position to improve that work. As leaders, we needed to fix the problems out of Max's reach. As leaders, we have a broader reach. If we had missed the opportunity to watch Max and speak with him, we would not have understood the source of added waste or the potential point of the introduction of product defects. Gemba is important because it facilitated the observation, communication, understanding, and resolution of a real problem. We didn't complify the problem by trying to solve it by mandate or at a distance.

The process problem that Max so clearly illustrated for us was ultimately addressed by putting a production line spotter in place to prepare the glass carts in sequence. The impact of putting the right glass on the right carts nearest to the glazer resulted in a 30 percent cycle time improvement. So, when we improve our processes, we are improving cycle time, waste, and profit. When we use observable data to streamline our processes, we not only cut waste but also drive employee satisfaction. These improvements lead to customer satisfaction with quality products delivered on time. This is how we create a culture that allows us to remove impediments not just for the sake of profits but for the sake of all the stakeholders.

When we lead by example, the culture shifts. After Max's experience, plant leaders did more exercises like this. In each instance, cycle times improved. Just as importantly, each time employee engagement, customer satisfaction, and the culture of the manufacturing site improved. Additionally, leaders learned that stopping and watching, then talking to the people who do the work, yields many opportunities to coach teams to improve and develop into proactive problem-solvers.

> *Asking questions is how to continue learning and get to the root of issues. However, if you stop learning because you're afraid of looking like you don't know everything, you are essentially creating a culture where fear is more important than knowledge.*

While the actions themselves seem simple and the results are compelling, we return to the idea of knowing yourself. Sometimes, leaders are fearful that they don't know exactly what to do or how to do it and do not want to make problems worse or look foolish for trying something new. If you really want to decomplify your leadership style, you need to show up where the value is created and get comfortable with being uncomfortable.

You must be ok with not having all the answers if you ever hope to know what you don't know. To be fair, we are taught throughout our lives to answer questions, not necessarily how to ask them. In fact, we are often rewarded for the best answers with grades in school or promotions at work. Asking questions is how to continue to learn and get to the root of issues. However, if you stop learning because you're afraid of looking like you don't know everything, you are essentially creating a culture where fear is more important than knowledge. Asking questions, being curious, engaging associates, and providing resources so that associates are empowered to make things better and solve problems are all signs of strong leaders who put the success of the organization ahead of their own egos.

Now, let's discuss what leadership could have gotten wrong with Max's example. First, what if leaders stayed in their offices and never visited the factory floor at all? The only indicators we could get that there was a problem with the glazer carts would come from product managers complaining about incomplete orders or customers complaining about lead times. Perhaps we saw the inability to keep staffing levels up in the factory because of frustrated workers. These symptoms have a direct path back to the glazer carts being understocked, out of sequence, or inaccessible.

The solution of placing a spotter on the glazer carts was a temporary measure until the supply chain issues could be resolved. We knew this was process debt because it was a temporary fix, but it was also a first step in helping Max and improving efficiency. Knowingly accepting some process debt as an intermediary to a full solution is an appropriate response, as it demonstrates both the dedication to resolve the larger issues *and* brings about some short-term benefits. The observation and first efforts to improve Max's challenges made us more aware and sensitive to impacts on the factory floor, so we could intervene should other shortfalls occur.

Let's say leadership never met Max, but they know they have a problem with incomplete deliveries or product quality based on a variety of indicators. Perhaps the service desk is receiving increased calls about manufacturing defects. Maybe sales data are showing increased lost sales, but it is not obvious why that is. Leadership might be chasing these metrics all over the company in support, sales, and marketing and trying to fix a problem they don't understand. Every attempt they make to solve the wrong problem just adds complexity and complifies the business further.

What are some reactionary responses that leaders make when faced with bad news? When sales drop, leaders spend money on marketing and advertising, offer discounts, or pressure employees to sell more. When faced with product quality issues, they beat up or switch suppliers, blame standards, or pressure employees to do better. When management receives complaints about incomplete orders, they hold shipments, hire more people, and pressure employees to do better.

Not one of these efforts would ever fix the fact that glass shortages from suppliers are adding time, waste, and employee stress to the manufacturing process. Rather, each of these traditional and reactionary fixes is complifying and obscuring the root of a very fixable problem and adding new problems to the mix. No one is motivated by hearing that they aren't trying hard enough. Instead, leaders need to go and see, learn, and assist as appropriate.

Decomplified leadership happens when leaders genuinely listen and seek richer observations rather than relying on a handful of metrics. Rely on fresh eyes and fresh perspectives to find opportunities for continuous improvement. When they exclusively trust numbers without questioning their deeper meaning, leadership blatantly complifies the situation and probably makes it worse. No single key performance indicator (KPI) would be as valuable as an hour of watching Max and then speaking with him. Relying too heavily on KPIs, especially the wrong KPIs, is a weak form of management, not leadership. An entire data transformation with all the best analytics might lead you to the problem factory, but once there, you need to stop, watch, and talk to the workers to understand *how* things work before you can hope to make them work better.

Max's predicament might only count for a fraction of the total corporate waste or customer satisfaction. However, the benefits of *understanding* Max's problem include both leading by example and learning from examples.

Decomplifying the issue of misaligned glazer carts was as simple as realigning the availability and sequence of the glass with the orders. It was as simple as that. Simple, however, doesn't mean easy. It is not easy to get leaders out of their comfort zones and into the line of fire with their products and their employees. Wisdom does not thrive in comfort zones, complacency does. Complacency is the breeding ground for complification. The lesson with Max's story is that decomplification benefits from active listening and direct observation. These actions may seem passive, but they are not; they are strategic rather than reactionary. They are simple, but they are not easy.

Leaders who strive to decomplify their approach seek the whole picture to gain deeper insight and avoid unintended consequences. Most KPIs measure how an organization *is performing*, not necessarily how it accomplishes its work. The following is an example of *how* a great leader contributes to a great company by changing *how* she does things to improve how the company is doing.

Julidar Amiruddin, a general manager in Indonesia, oversees 1,400 employees at plants in Jakarta and Cirebon. She is responsible for the Indonesia business, and she begins each morning with a thirty minute meeting with 120 of her leaders to discuss daily management. Julidar *could* just collect metrics, have the top leaders report, and have direct conversations about goals and objectives. Instead of focusing exclusively on numbers, Julidar dedicates her morning leadership meeting to focusing on how the leadership is living the company's values. She drives a qualitative daily appraisal of the company's culture.

Julidar also instituted a thirty-minute weekly training program for members of her team to share information that will help each other hone their leadership skills. She does not preach to her team; she asks them to testify to the techniques that work, take ownership, and share lessons for efforts that fail. This openness breeds trust and builds knowledge.

Her team has also provided daily and weekly training opportunities for every associate to build their skills. The opportunities are not limited to the job they have today but includes their aspirations. Whether associates want to learn English, learn to use MS Office products, or learn how to provide customer service, the route to learning and growth is wide open for all. The cost to her company is twenty minutes a day that they are reinvesting in her associates. The reward is the most engaged and productive work force in the company.

The Indonesian leadership team spends nearly one-third of their working hours on employee engagement, from eating lunch with associates to investing time in hallway conversations to get to know them as people. Building culture is a commitment, not an afterthought. These efforts can be measured with a KPI: Julidar's 1,400 associates report an employee engagement score of 84 percent, which is outstanding and significantly higher than the global average for all manufacturers. Then, the correlation of employee engagement scores with customer satisfaction scores shows us how to measure what really matters.

Engaged associates are productive associates. While the trend of *quiet quitting* has made headlines in recent times, the truth is people have always experienced burnout. Engagement is the antidote to burnout and the key to sustained productivity. The proof of Julidar's efforts is in her results. Her teams always make their goals and they do not struggle with productivity in the ways that other teams who have lower engagement scores struggle to make their goals.

You can't move the needle by guessing what drives a gauge. To see results, you need to affect change by taking action. Some of the things you try might fail, but not trying is to resign yourself to failure. Julidar is affecting change and driving a cultural shift through leadership, not management. Her simplicity takes the form of routine and regular conversation and actions that are never deprioritized because she understands that to set aside these efforts is to abandon the strategies she has committed to for her associates and the company. This is Julidar's standard work.

Just like standard work defines manufacturing processes and functional capabilities, leaders should define their own standard work. Leader standard work must be aligned with delivering the decomplified objectives of the enterprise and devoid of wasteful activities. Your own *leader standard work* needs to specify those actions and pursuits that subscribe to the definition of a great company and the Four Absolutes. We can define leader standard work that will ensure that time, resources, and attention are directed toward stimulating rather than stifling organizational success.

> *Leader standard work must be aligned with delivering the decomplified objectives of the enterprise and devoid of wasteful activities.*

The success in these examples comes directly from active listening, which is an incredibly important skill to have in order to succeed in any leadership role. Developing strong active listening skills involves taking time to really hear what someone is saying and responding thoughtfully. This can mean asking open-ended questions to draw out more information, repeating back what the other person has said to ensure understanding, and providing nonverbal cues that indicate you are listening and engaged. Active listening can help to simplify complex issues by providing more clarity on the underlying issues and identifying potential solutions.

Leaders are trained their whole lives to answer questions and solve problems. It is how we are rewarded and promoted. Much of what is demonstrated in the decomplified leadership approach is all about creating a problem-solving culture and asking questions. Asking questions with sincerity and drawing on the collective knowledge and engagement of customers and associates alike.

Active listening in a proactive manner, like Julidar's standard work entails, is one method. Another is actively engaging and listening in real time, like in Max's production line example. Then there are the more difficult conversations, where active listening objectively matters the most.

One of the hardest things for any leader is the reduction of resources and associated cost cutting exercises. At the beginning of the pandemic, we decided to use furloughs rather than permanently terminating associates. Furloughs are not ideal, as there are long stretches where employees have unpaid and unplanned time off work; however, they will have a job to return to at the end of the furlough.

Furloughs tend to protect jobs and benefits for the employee, even though pay and amount of work are reduced. This, in turn, allows the company to retain talented and experienced associates. No one knew how business was going to be affected by the pandemic, so the choice to use furloughs as an option to prevent losses was made early. Fortunately, that year would post very good results in the end.

Yet, it seemed inherently unfair to post those results without rewarding the associates who had given up pay and work to remain with the company during uncertain times. They had invested their faith and futures in the company. We offered a onetime bonus at the end of the year, which was intended to return the money forfeited during the furloughs.

The reaction was amazing, and associates were thankful for the bonus. However, they also communicated that the furlough choice was appreciated because of the mutual risk and stability it offered over a job cut. When associates learned they would be paid back lost wages, they felt the gesture set us apart from other employers. Their enthusiasm underscored the company's values and the greatness of being a place people wanted to work.

Engagement remained high for a long time. This action was more than expected, improved our ability and alignment going forward, and built so much good will. The engagement survey conducted during the year of the furlough showed an improvement over the prior year, even with the furlough. This was a good indication of the value people put on the furlough choice over a reduction in workers. The payback bonuses secured that engagement, which continued to grow.

In the stories of Max, Julidar, and the pandemic furloughs, leadership is listening, learning, and acting in ways that have a direct effect on building a great company. They are not focusing on just customers, employees, or investors, but building a strong culture that promotes the interests of all three. In these stories, the actors are eliminating existing process debt and avoiding future process debt by removing the impediments of faulty processes and clearing the way for open communication, which drives customer satisfaction, employee engagement, and the value of the company itself. It's the value of the company that appeals to investors, so being able to communicate that value at every level of the organization drives a cohesive message that investors appreciate. When everyone in an organization can be aligned in understanding and explaining the same message, the organization is poised to achieve results.

One effective technique to drive that cohesive message is a monthly open mic opportunity for anyone engaged in problem solving to bring their problem to a global call. In that forum, associates could share a problem they solved successfully for everyone's benefit or could raise a problem they are working on and share the process while seeking coaching or guidance from everyone on the call. This is a safe, Socratic opportunity to share, receive help, and learn as an organization. Being either a seeker or provider in these forums—

sometimes both—raised engagement and brought fresh perspectives for all concerned.

The value of *go see, go learn, and engage* informed my leader standard work as a CEO, which was specific with weekly, monthly, and quarterly actions allocated to going to Gemba, performance management, critical strategic decisions, and customer, associate, and investor engagement. This approach paralleled the definition of a great company. Interestingly, the disproportionate time allocation and most frequent items in my standard work relate to going to Gemba, associate development, communication, and engagement.

Think about decomplifying your leadership:

❑ *Does your organization have a rallying cry? If so, does it capture the promise and purpose of the work your organization does?*

❑ *Do you routinely visit where the value is created in your value stream? Do you seek fresh perspectives to evaluate and improve the performance at different levels of the organization? What can you do in your standard work to ensure alignment in these areas?*

❑ *Are you able to define your own leader standard work? Do your associates understand, and are they able to explain their own standard work? As an individual, what can you do to better align your standard work with organizational success? As a leader, what actions can you take to ensure that standard work is understood at all levels of the organization?*

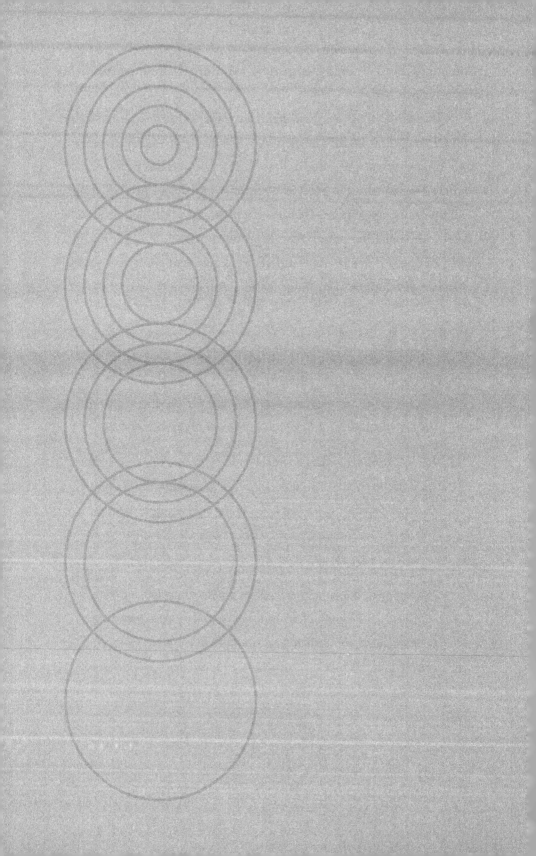

2.

Fresh Eyes and Clear Voices

High performing teams promote a culture of honesty, authenticity and safe conflict.

—JAMES KERR

A rallying cry is a powerful tool that leaders should embrace to communicate and motivate their people to deliver on the mission of their organization. Beneath the rallying cry lies the values that shape the mission and drive the culture that achieves it. Just as cultures change and evolve to meet the needs of the customers and marketplaces they serve, the rallying cry can also change to help align the organization and maintain motivation to deliver desired outcomes.

The rallying cry is an expression of the organization's values and the goals of the organizational culture. What are your organizational values? Do your people know, understand, and subscribe to those values? Does the organizational culture reflect and serve those values? Decomplifying means removing any process or ambiguity that obscures the values of your organization or threatens the health of a culture that reflects and serves those values. Now, let's explore how a leader builds and maintains a culture through decomplification.

Your organizational culture is the garden where all the elements of a great company thrive. In a healthy culture, your associates want to work with and for you, investors want to invest in you, and customers want to buy from you because you delight customers with both your differentiated and superior customer service and your products.

Just like in the natural world, your cultural habitat is impacted by the elements. Your values are the elements that sustain your cultural environment. Values are the air, water, energy, and nourishment that make a healthy cultural experience possible. If those values are corrupted at any point, the entire culture is threatened. Values can be corrupted willfully or negligently. Values are corrupted when they are not understood, honored, reinforced, or practiced. However, when values are held true and put into practice, your culture will flourish.

In his book, *The Culture Code*, Daniel Coyle introduces three habits or skills that are prevalent in all healthy and productive cultures. Those are safety, vulnerability, and purpose.[5] If your organization can translate those skills into your core values, then you will be heading in the right direction. However, the other values of your organization will inform both your purpose and how you behave as an organization.

Your values shape the culture, and your culture can change to fit the circumstances of the changing world without threatening or disagreeing with your core values. For instance, prior to the Great Recession in 2008, Club Car, Inc. was the iconic and market leading brand in golf cars. The company and its people were globally renown in the golf industry, and their products for the golf course led the market in quality, performance, and style.

Club Car's company tagline, plastered on their truck fleet and advertising, was "The Global Leader in Golf." The corporate offices resembled a retro-style golf clubhouse in color palette, artwork, and furnishings. Associates were encouraged to actively support the game.

---

5   Daniel Coyle, *The Culture Code: The Secrets of Highly Successful Groups* (Bantam, 2018).

Participation in the company golf league was encouraged, and lessons were provided for those not yet familiar with golf.

Their values were aligned with the Four Absolutes—they were clearly obsessed with their customers at Club Car. When associates went above and beyond, they were said to "bleed black and gold," which are the corporate colors, so strong and prevalent was their service-oriented culture. They were also invested in fielding the right team, training them, and helping them fit their culture. They obviously delivered results, which made them the undisputed global leader. They also owned their dependencies and delivered exceptional service, products, and market performance. Everything was perfect for Club Car's culture to deliver on their mission to retain their title as the global leader, but only in golf.

As you can imagine, most of the investment at Club Car was directed at golf related products and marketing. However, market and growth pressures prompted a desire to market Club Car products for other applications outside of golf.

Yet, this motivation to grow in other areas ran counter to the expression of Club Car's culture. Consider that employees whose objectives were tied to expanding beyond golf applications had titles like "Golf and Utility Sales," "Golf and Commercial Business Development," and "Golf and Consumer Channel Leader." Clearly, everyone at Club Car still had a foot in, and perhaps their hearts and minds, in the all-important golf space.

With everyone still grounded in golf and with the importance of golf reinforced continuously in every aspect of the company, including titles and business cards, the challenge of their own alignment was enormous. Innovation, resources, and investments were dispropor-tionately focused on golf. This is a great example of having emotion for *what we do*, but if they wanted to do more, the extreme expression of that passion was a liability.

31

The strategic intent was there. Unfortunately, the motivation to change and the commitment to do so were not evident. People, resources, and investment were not fully committed. The question remained whether this strategy was critical, important, or just desirable. The fact was that the very people charged with moving Club Car away from its reliance on golf were still wedded to golf. The business and its associates had not yet found the enthusiasm for *doing what needed to be done*. That was about change along with the culture.

At the height of the real estate bubble and ensuing financial crisis, many declared golf course real estate dead. The golf market suffered immensely with fewer rounds played, club memberships cancelled, and golf course closings outpacing new golf course openings.

Imminent decline in the core golf business provided the burning platform to transform the business and develop new growth vectors. The motivation and newfound enthusiasm to be *more than golf* ensued.

The first order of business was structuring the business so that objectives and resources were exclusively committed to new categories. Club Car could remain the global leader in golf, but they also needed to direct dedicated energy toward growth beyond golf. In that vein, a commercial vehicle group and a consumer vehicle group were established, staffed with full-time associates, and elevated to report right next to the legacy golf business. The equivalence was key to changing the culture to include new markets.

To be sure, this very visible act of separation may have been one of the hardest cultural acts at Club Car. Even with the challenges in the golf business and a foundational understanding of the need for change, the cultural pull was to stick with the legacy business.

While there was plenty of experience and expertise in the golf vehicle space, including product and engineering, channel, and customer, it turned out that there were significant gaps in capabilities to successfully expand into the commercial and consumer spaces. What had been an aspiration to expand and grow outside of golf was never set up for execution. New people with related expertise were required, and new capabilities in engineering, manufacturing, and the like would be required to be successful. This is where the second absolute impacted culture—they had to field the right team.

What was once viewed as just a product and channel play to sell existing products to new customers took on a whole new meaning as new opportunities were identified and studied. The studied approach yielded opportunities in commercial and consumer areas that would require new product development to supplement the current offerings, new distribution channels, and even new design and manufacturing capabilities. This was how Club Car genuinely owned their dependencies.

The critical strategic decision process allowed for data to be consolidated to determine where to play, how to win, and what capabilities would be required to be successful. The transformation led to Club Car holding on to its market leader status in golf vehicles *while also* successfully expanding its reach into commercial and consumer vehicles. This included the development of a 4X4 ATV product line, the first on-road low-speed electric vehicle offering, and a significant upgrade and expansion of utility and people transport vehicle lineups.

The technical, product development, and manufacturing developments did not present the biggest challenge or innovation for Club Car. The real challenge would prove to be channel access. In the case of the ATV lineup, utilizing current channel partners would prove to be limiting. Current channel partners, much like Club Car itself, were primarily focused on golf. Studies also showed that customers were not likely to associate the Club Car brand with the ATV product line, and in fact, the brand did not match the attributes of a rugged work vehicle. Even with a more appropriate brand, the channel issue would be expensive and insurmountable.

Interestingly enough, the studies exposed brands that may be more successful marketing an ATV work vehicle alongside other products. The critical strategic decision for Club Car was, rather than invest in a new brand and channel which is expensive and time consuming, becoming an original equipment manufacturer (OEM). Club Car sold their 4X4 ATV work vehicles to other companies that had channel access with their own equipment but needed a work vehicle and 4x4 lineup to augment it. In other words, Club Car partnered with companies who already had channel access and brand credibility but chose not to invest in the innovation and development of these new products. OEM in this space may be more expedient and profitable. They needed to focus on delivering results, and that meant finding the right channel.

This decision to enter a partnership allowed Club Car to leverage its capabilities, resources, and deep expertise in light vehicle design and manufacturing while relying on partners to leverage existing channels, marketing, and branding. It takes vulnerability and vision over ego to recognize the immense value of partnerships over controlling and creating everything in-house.

It takes vulnerability and vision over ego to recognize the immense value of partnerships.

When Club Car chose to partner, they were practicing the decomplified absolute of owning dependencies and addressing them in a way that best met the needs of shareholders to enter the market faster. They also served their customers by providing a superior product. Market partnerships allow a business to accelerate access to the marketplace while learning how to navigate and target select offerings over time.

Club Car's partnership ultimately allowed them to produce product for multiple brands and benefit from greater volume than they would have from a single brand. They also benefited from this growth much sooner and with far less marketing and logistical investment than their own brand and an unproven and limited initial channel approach on their own. Club Car ended up with a new product line and could develop its channels to market at its own speed. The OEM partners were able to offer a branded product line without the investment in development and manufacturing.

By changing strategically while retaining their values of customer relationships, quality products, team engagement, and market leadership, Club Car made the leap to a new business model that worked better in the economic reality they faced in the early 2000s. It is one thing to say you *want* to change, and something entirely different to make change. Without aligning the people in their organization, the culture could not absorb the necessary changes to respond to the market and grow their business.

Once Club Car understood that they had to put their money where their mouths were with talent and innovation, they made the necessary changes to both support and build the right team, develop new products, and build the success that would make them a global leader in golf, consumer, and commercial light vehicles. This evolution in culture allowed Club Car to grow in new areas but didn't diminish the strong customer focus or innovation drive in their core golf business. Through internal innovation and partnerships, they were able to solve problems for golf customers, too, and deliver a new and expanded customer experience called Visage™.

Club Car's culture still bleeds black and gold. The best essentials of their culture did not change; the culture just expanded to include more customers, markets, and internal assets. Their position as a global leader is based on how they built and held onto market share, profitability, and stakeholder satisfaction.

The Club Car example is important because if leadership doesn't appreciate what their associates are up against in making changes, change cannot happen. In my career, my standard work included a number of activities that were designed to identify and communicate areas of opportunity, accelerate change, and share development across the organization. One method came straight out of childhood, the domain where people are naturally positioned and inclined to learn.

Throughout my tenure as a leader, I hosted a Summer reading program (SRP). The purpose of SRP is to use a book club format to help stimulate the organization toward new concepts or opportunities, reinforce significant needs, and participate in shared learning and development. The ultimate goal of the SRP was to understand and improve how to deliver results, obsess about customers, own dependencies, and field the right team to become a great company. In June of each year, I would announce the book for SRP and provide it to the extended leadership team. We would also schedule a session in August, usually with the author, to discuss the book and how its topic related to the business. The outcome of the SRP typically influences culture by stimulating discussion, internal thought leadership, and new insights, and the initial leadership team would often bring the book and the ideas to their own teams, disseminating the ideas and a common language throughout the company as a whole.

One of the early SRP selections was *Multipliers* by Liz Wiseman.[6] Wiseman cited leadership research that identified *multipliers* as those leaders who were inclusive and collaborative and whose style and

---

6   Liz Wiseman and Greg McKeown, *Multipliers: How the Best Leaders Make Everyone Smarter* (Harper Collins, 2010).

approach made people around them better performers, while diminishers, whose operational approach tended to be more closed off and secretive, have a style that diminishes those they work with. Wiseman's premise is that individuals who perform as multipliers stimulate two times more out of the people they lead than diminishers do. Multipliers doubled the intelligence and capability of their organization without adding headcount, and multipliers contribute to increasing people's intelligence. This seemed like a decomplified and lean approach to leadership, and in retrospect, this really is at the core of why I subscribe to SRP as a cultural leadership tool.

The effect of SRP helped change or strengthen the culture everywhere I put it to use. It created a common language for patterns and processes we could adopt, adapt, or eliminate. In the best situations, it reinforced an existing culture, and in every event, the group learned about the real culture and concerns in each organization through collaboration and open communication. The reading program also brought fresh eyes into each session as leaders shared their own stories and learned from each other about what was happening in their own company and culture.

Personally, I learned a lot in each SRP session beyond just the actual content. SRPs are a healthy feedback loop to build understanding about how real culture expresses itself through a variety of filters. Those filters are the unique perspectives each thought leader brings through their research, experiences, observations, and insights. Collectively, the SRP is a powerful tool that brings together unique ways of examining and improving our own behavior and, in turn, the culture as a whole.

Shaping this kind of learning and growth is an intentional action that flies in the face of process debt. It's always easier to *not* read a book and *not* have these conversations. It's easier to have fewer meetings and to focus only on the essential execution of business operations. It is not, however, easy to fix a disengaged culture. It is not easy to become a company people want to work at, buy from, and invest in if the actions of the organization do not demonstrate a growth mindset. This is a deficiency that is difficult to repair, so it is better to proactively invest in that growth because it will reveal both obstacles *and* opportunities.

When we used *The Amazon Way* for the first time at Trane, I expected the four principles that I've adopted as the Decomplified Absolutes to be the most valuable to the leadership team. While they did appreciate and get on board with those absolutes, they surprised me with their enthusiasm in discussing an Amazon principle that I didn't personally find as insightful. The leadership team and many of their own teams felt that the two pizza principle revealed a great deal about organizational culture.

The two pizza principle essentially posits that no team should be larger than can be satisfied with two pizzas, and by keeping teams smaller and communication clear, leaders can invest trust and authority in their team members. The Trane team strongly felt that the elements of empowerment and trust were not where they could be with our teams, and that was a revelation to me about where and how we needed to make changes. Furthermore, I learned that by listening to what resonated with others was the best way to understand behaviors I didn't directly observe.

As the participants in my extended leadership team were interacting with the author and each other, they highlighted an area of our culture that I was blind to. This area could very well have derailed any change and growth efforts we wanted to implement. That reality was clearly weighing on the team, unbeknownst to me. The book is a catalyst, and the program is the experiment. It is the result of the

SRP experience that stimulates organizational learning and growth and stimulates a thriving culture.

Summer reading programs are one method. Other companies use mentoring circles with similar success in stimulating creative and critical thinking with their leadership. While both methods are great means to stimulate leadership conversation, the culture includes the full organization, so it's crucial to engage the rest of your workforce to improve and sustain culture.

In my experience, listening to your associates is far more effective in creating a healthy culture than talking at them. Two modes I value for measuring cultural health and improving outcomes are fresh eyes and clear voices. Both methods require incorporating Coyle's skills of practicing safety and vulnerability and placing those values at the center of our culture.

Fresh eyes is the concept of welcoming new perspectives and approaches to a problem or situation. Typically, the eyes belong to an outsider who is new to the company, role, or activity being observed.

The fresh eyes approach is exactly what it sounds like. It relies on a safe environment from the very beginning of a person's tenure to create a space where "if you see something, say something," and celebrates the refreshing honesty of drawing everyone's attention to what needs to be better understood and possibly improved. Fresh eyes can help see the forest in spite of the trees and find the blind spots that people have accepted over time. Fresh eyes works best when leaders listen to what new or freshly assigned people observe about their new environment.

I've always made it a point as part of my standard work to engage with all the new hires and early career talent each quarter.

Every quarter, I would meet with people who had joined during the quarter. These meetings are very simple, and I make only a few brief comments welcoming them, revisiting our values, vision, and rallying cry, and explaining the reasons for having these sessions. I ask each participant to introduce themselves briefly and share where they have come from and what brought them to our company. I ask them to share their expectations and how reality has played out so far on their journey. Also, I ask them to provide something they have seen that may be an opportunity for us to improve. I genuinely welcome and appreciate the fresh perspectives of the people who can reflect an unfiltered and unjaded view of the company.

As with Max, the window assembler, and his glass picking challenges, fresh eyes are in play when I visit a plant and tend to see things that people in the plant walk by every day as they don't notice the abnormality or opportunity because it has become part of the landscape. However, the things I do notice are not evidence that I am smarter or wiser than anyone else. Rather, when experiencing a change of scenery, individuals and teams gain a fresh perspective. I also used a modification of fresh perspectives for leaders new to their roles. I ask them to briefly report out on observations early in their tenure, usually within ninety days, as these are the purest uptakes and a highly prized opportunity to see through their fresh eyes.

Fresh eyes work really well with new hires, associates at the beginning of their careers, and people in new roles. After serving in one position or location for a significant amount of time, individuals become so inured to the environment that they no longer question why or how the organization does certain things. It's no different from those common experiences of driving home and having no distinct memory of milestones we see every day on any particular day. When adding fresh eyes and, importantly, encouraging open communication, those people will ask questions and bring the attention back to the environment and established behaviors that may be opportunities for improvement, innovation, or efficiency. Going to Gemba is one example of leadership bringing fresh eyes to the line, but if practiced more broadly, an organization can constantly improve performance and eliminate waste. Fresh eyes are crucial to decomplifying a culture and how individuals express it.

New employees are particularly valuable because great efforts are made to teach them the values and cultural expectations, and they will notice when what is done doesn't agree with what is said. For instance, a new employee who learned all the physical safety standards is more likely to notice a missing fire extinguisher or a broken lock than the people who have walked by them every day for months.

One of the most dangerous phrases in business is *because that's how we always did it.* It's a pat response for any process, but it is also an excuse not to change. When you use the fresh eyes approach, that response is not allowed. When fresh eyes ask why or how something is done, if the culture cannot respond with clarity, then there is a problem and an opportunity to decomplify.

> *One of the most dangerous phrases in business is because that's how we always did it.*

Trane had long enjoyed a strong market position and associated profitability by owning the premium end of the residential HVAC market. They had great products. They boasted the best efficiencies and the best reliability. Their tagline falls into the iconic realm—"It's Hard to Stop a Trane." Trane Residential's standard work was entirely directed toward enhancing the efficiency and reliability of the product. They did it well, commanded premium pricing, and were the undisputed upmarket leader. You could say that the internal rallying cry at Trane was "The Premium Brand" and that their values included satisfying customers, improving the world, and benefitting shareholders.

The way they did this before the market changed worked for them. They satisfied the customer with the most reliable products. They served the world with more efficient products. They benefitted stakeholders with superior products that led the market and increased profitability.

Unfortunately, during the Great Recession, just like Club Car, Trane Residential suffered impacts on consumer market conditions, and performance was significantly affected. The market had changed, and the company hadn't responded in kind. In fact, the market had been changing for some time but may have gone unnoticed at Trane. More than likely, the change was acknowledged, but given the success of the company and the focus on reliability and efficiency, it was not viewed as significant. What had worked so well for so long was their magic formula.

When the economic downturn came, people sought to replace their systems only when necessary and at the lowest cost possible. The change meant that people were no longer able to buy the very best at the same rate, and Trane really didn't have a competitive product to offer. They needed to change now.

At first, the change in market demand toward lower efficiency solutions was misunderstood. Trane believed that everyone really should understand the need for better efficiency, which would save money for customers in the long run, rather than simply lowering first cost. The ethos was the noble approach to offering Trane's elevated perception of quality, efficiency, and performance rather than the decreased first cost through lower efficiency. They believed their value was reliability and efficiency, so they continued to develop more efficient equipment. Putting their resources toward and doubling down on what had worked in the past did not yield benefits in the present. As they discounted the sustainability of the lower efficiency and price point (often called entry level) products, competitors grew.

While Trane focused on the best efficiency and the best reliability, they weren't prepared to develop products and sell at the entry level. To meet the change in market by a change in behavior, Trane had to rally the entire business around changing what was in their hearts and blood. Everything would have to change including product management, marketing and sales and supply chain. The team discovered a new internal rallying cry that, evolved and changed along with their culture and product offerings. This new rallying cry highlighted the need to change the focus from exclusively the premium, high efficiency marketplace, which was now shrinking, to the broader market, including entry level.

Trane Residential needed to have "a product for every home." This became the rallying cry that propelled the company to revamp its product offering, including the launch of a new fighter brand. It also allowed it to rethink how to best restructure its lineup at the premium end to ensure that it did not lose its leadership position there. Trane was so effective at living up to its tagline and their premium focus that they struggled with designing a competitive entry-level product line. They used their *absolute* idea of quality and reliability to build products that cost too much to sell at entry level and were not competitive. It was difficult to leave that mindset. When the company looked at competitive offerings and evaluated how best to get to market quickly, it became apparent that partnering to purchase an OEM product that could be branded was the efficient solution to get to market profitably and begin the process of changing the internal concept of what is possible.

While Club Car became the OEM to meet changing market demands and learn the marketing channels they needed to enter, Trane had the marketing channels and purchased the OEM product to keep up with market demand. Both businesses used strategic partnerships to give their cultures time to learn, adapt, and grow into their new identities.

Trane learned from their OEM product that not only could they create a lower price point product themselves, but they could do it even better. "A product for every home" worked for a few years to rally the company to transform its product line and channel capabilities to meet a changing marketplace. Once that was ingrained in the culture, it became evident that it was time to focus on the next aspiration. Trane Residential now had the capabilities to serve a broader marketplace and wanted to regain its position at the top.

The rallying cry changed to reflect the new battle. The new rallying cry, "the undeniable market leader," embodied the spirit to not only be the leader in premium markets but to lead across all categories of residential HVAC. This rallying cry motivated the entire business. It informed how everyone was measured, what goals were deployed, and where investments and innovations were made to further the cause. The results speak for themselves, as Trane Residential enjoyed market share gains every quarter for over four years while delivering industry benchmark returns.[7] The rallying cry alone did not drive market share. However, the excitement, alignment, and commitment that the rallying cry drove delivered innovation in products, operations, and customer relationships that propelled Trane residential to greatness.

---

7   Trane Technologies, "2017 Ingersoll Rand Investor & Analyst Day," Trane Technologies, May 10, 2017, https://investors.tranetechnologies.com/news-and-events/events/event-details/2017/2017-Ingersoll-Rand-Investor--Analyst-Day/default.aspx.

Bellowing a rallying cry from every mountaintop will not magically grow your revenue and profitability, no matter how well it is written and communicated. There has to be a solid bridge from aspiration to execution. The clarity of leadership needs to marry the purpose of corporate culture for a rallying cry to provide the emotional link to the *why*.

The Trane Residential team subscribed to being the leader as defined—growing the top line ahead of competition and expanding margins—with the express objective to be the undeniable leader. Recognizing that regaining market share was key to this aspiration, the measurement currency needed to match.

Since market share is measured in units, every decision, every investment, and every objective were denominated in how many incremental units they would generate. Market share became part of the language and the culture to tie everything to units. Annual operating plans started with a determination of how much market share could be gained in the year and how many incremental units would be needed to achieve that goal. Unit goals then cascaded into every aspect of the planning process of the business. Supply chains were set, people were hired, and investments were made based on delivering the incremental units required to meet the market share growth objective. Everyone in the business was keenly aware of their part and their commitment to Trane Residential becoming "the undeniable market leader."

Leadership clarity, like in this example from Trane, is directly related to the clear voices approach. It's one thing to be clear in your leadership messaging, but if you are unclear in your *leadership listening*, you're only talking at people, not really communicating. Chick-fil-A is a fast-food restaurant, but they train their crew on the basics of communication, including the concepts of noise and feedback. They also teach their employees to paraphrase to ensure they understand their customers *and* their leaders and crewmates alike.

The clear voices strategy emphasizes the importance of effective communication and messaging. The goal of this strategy is to remove any unnecessary noise or distraction in organizational and interpersonal communication that is likely to cause confusion or misunderstanding.

Using the clear voices strategy requires removing the *noise* that disrupts clarity and causes confusion. Noise complifies, clarity decomplifies. Like fresh eyes, you don't shoot the messenger. While the fresh eyes approach is all about bringing in novel perspectives, clear voices appreciate all perspectives. Later in the book is a great example of using clear voices to change the culture in the associate's experience, but as a cultural practice.

In my experience, town halls serve the communication model because leaders don't speak *at* the workforce; they engage the associates as a team. Again, leadership must create that safe environment and practice vulnerability and humility, where they admit they can be wrong and that even or especially leaders can fail just like everyone else. This is part of how people learn together and grow sustainably. Defensiveness and arrogance are noise; they complify the culture and need to be weeded out to allow for clear voices to ring true and deliver the messages that sustain a healthy culture and serve the values of an organization.

A clear voices approach is mutually beneficial. The premise is based on the faith that the workforce has a unique and engaged perspective that is worthy of hearing. Moreover, the workforce should be comfortable and compelled to share their valuable perspectives for the benefit of their own satisfaction, the well-being of their coworkers and the company, and the good of the customer.

I believe town halls are very effective in communicating messages, reinforcing culture and values, soliciting feedback, and sharing recognition. Recognition can be both a public and private method for reinforcing cultural norms. Town halls tend to be heavier on presentation, with time for questions and comments at the end. I have always made it a practice to take as many questions and comments in real time as is feasible. You never know what you're going to learn in a town hall, and you have to be prepared to hear a comment beneath a question.

Once, earlier in my career, we announced in a town hall meeting that the facility was going fully nonsmoking. One of the people in the Q&A session stood up and thanked the leadership for going smoke-free, and then asked, "When will we become a drug-free workplace?"

In the manufacturing space, drug abuse is dangerous for the employee, their coworkers, the company, the customers, and the shareholders alike. There is no place for it, and yet here was someone in

Town halls are very effective in communicating messages, reinforcing culture and values, soliciting feedback, and sharing recognition.

a production facility telling us, boldly, that we had a serious problem. While we could answer the comment disguised as a question that day by reinforcing the drugfree policy and safety rules and reminding associates of the programs we had in place, like the Employee Assistance Program (EAP), we owed the associate not just an answer but gratitude for speaking the truth.

While this question was unique, many times, even in the best cultures, associates may not be comfortable speaking in front of a large group to leadership, so I also made room for questions and comments submitted after the session, and my leadership team was dedicated to answering all questions, even days after the town hall. Yet, there is always a need to hear the voices of the workforce and reinforce respect for their perspectives. So, we added another session, held at a different time, called "Ask Me Anything." While town halls are probably 80/20 presentation and message to Q&A and comments, "Ask Me Anything" was the reverse with a brief comments session, and the majority was dedicated to hearing what's on people's minds.

Regardless of the forum, any opportunity like town halls, skip levels, or fresh eye visits to other sites can and should be utilized at all levels of an organization, not just at the enterprise or most seasoned levels. Fostering full, open, and safe communication and feedback is how to practice and model vulnerability.

Just as leaders need to listen to the clear voices and fresh eyed experiences of the associates, everyone in an organization needs to practice the same safety and vulnerability with customers and stake-holders. Customers who bother to call our service centers, write online reviews, or connect with us on social media channels should be recognized for their honesty. Rather than a knee-jerk reaction to criticism, practice reflection to understand the message and respond with authenticity. Listen, learn, and correct course to be true to our values and foster a healthy culture internally and externally to become consistent with your values and set your organization up for greatness.

Yes, the right thing is sometimes also the hard thing, but when it comes to sustainability, our values cannot be diverted for the easy road. Just as Club Car changed their business model and their culture to respond to market realities, sometimes what has always worked must change to deliver results. Failing to remove a rotting branch or weed out unhealthy practices doesn't serve the associates, customers, or stakeholders. Next, you will learn how to use these techniques and others to decomplify the experience of your associates.

Think about decomplifying your culture:

❑ *How do you recognize and resolve cultural impediments to your ability to execute your strategy and deliver results?*

❑ *Is your culture an asset or a liability? Do you and your team know the strengths and weaknesses of your current culture?*

❑ *How do you solicit feedback and ensure clear communication from all levels in your organization, and how can you do it better?*

❑ *How do you reinforce your strategic messages and align them with values to honor your purpose consistently and clearly as an organization?*

3. | Engage and Deliver

*Employees who believe that management is
concerned about them as a whole person—not
just an employee—are more productive, more
satisfied, more fulfilled. Satisfied employees mean
satisfied customers, which leads to profitability.*

—ANNE M. MULCAHY

B y now, you can see the importance of people in everything
leaders do to decomplify and build a great company. In great
companies, leaders understand the importance of attracting,
developing, placing, and retaining people to maximize performance. No
other activity is as important as fielding the right team and ensuring that
they are engaged and equipped to do their jobs to the best of their ability
in line with the organizational objectives. When leaders fail to shape
and mobilize the workforce, they forfeit the opportunity for greatness.

The creation and maintenance of a healthy talent pipeline are
crucial to the lifecycle of any successful business. A great business
prioritizes its talent pipeline. Through leadership and by building the
right culture, both the definition of a great company—one that people
want to buy from, work for, and invest in—and the Four Absolutes
specifically call out associates as critical to success. People want to
work for a great company because they believe in the purpose and

values of the company, feel their contributions are valued, and can realize their personal and career aspirations.

An engaged workforce takes ownership of their training and growth opportunities, and a great company makes those resources available, accessible, and the growth attainable to those motivated individuals. Often, leaders abdicate ownership of their associates' development, leaving the associates to navigate their growth alone. Leaders neglect talent pipeline maintenance at their own peril.

The importance of engaged associates is that they contribute to the Decomplified Absolutes to create a great company.

At an organizational level, the orchestration of a positive cultural shift relies on strong communication and actively listening to associates to ensure that the messages are being received, internalized, and affecting the necessary change. At the macro level, cultural health is an attribute of the company as a larger organism, but at the micro level, it is expressed in the relationships and behaviors of the individual members of the larger organization. You need to establish both the culture—as the climate where you can grow great people—and the interpersonal relationships that keep those people engaged and invested on a personal level.

The importance of engaged associates, who not only create and deliver the value of the enterprise but also equally derive benefits, is that they will contribute to the other Decomplified Absolutes and help you create a great company together. Of course, great people want to work with great people, and great people attract other great people. As you would expect, a great company must make attractive returns for its investors through operational excellence and sustainable productivity, but you cannot do that without engaged associates.

Clearly, practicing the decomplify absolute of fielding the right team is critical to delivering for your customers and delivering results. In a way, you can also consider that the absolutes are the way you ensure that your associates are integral to your organizational health and culture. If you change the lens and view the absolutes in relation to your associates and their experience, you obsess over your associates, surround them with

Great people want to work with great people, and great people attract other great people.

other great people (field the right team), wisely weigh your options, and ensure that you own the dependencies of developing and maintaining a talent pipeline and do what you say you will do (deliver results). The decomplified approach to leading the enterprise also describes the relationship with the very people you are dependent on for the success of your business.

To build the culture of always developing and pushing your good people, you need to focus on several key areas of opportunity. Creating the culture of continuous improvement in talent acquisition, development, placement, and retention must hit every part of the organization.

When transforming an organization, I typically start the focus in three key areas of the organization that help to move ahead the fastest. They include early career development, ready leadership talent, and the senior leader group. Focusing on the unique needs of these groups and aligning interests and opportunities that will be mutually beneficial to associates and the organization alike is a significant decomplifier for talent management.

Focusing on the early career group gives you the ability to bring in fresh perspectives and flexible minds and build up a strong stable of individual contributors with long-term potential. You're stocking your talent pipeline. An early leadership group enables you to maintain that talent pipeline and keep it healthy, while providing opportunities and motivation for the largest segment of the workforce.

When you have a clear and strategically aligned leadership career path available and the support and commitment to mobilize those early leaders, you energize and motivate the entire organization. It is one thing to bring these early leaders up the ranks, but it is another thing to keep challenging, growing, and engaging them at every level. You don't want to lose talent anywhere along the continuum of your pipeline because your execution will break down.

Finally, the senior leadership group benefits the entire organization by ensuring strategic alignment to maintain a synchronized order and ensure that the whole of the organization is in harmony. They really do set the tone for the enterprise, leading by example and being the engagement catalyst for everyone. Continuing to develop this group individually and as a leadership team pays dividends. By focusing consistently and in a coordinated way on these three groups within the talent pipeline, leaders decomplify the effort required for assessment, development, and placement. Leadership techniques from earlier in the book are relevant to developing and retaining individuals with high aptitude and positive attitudes in your talent pipeline.

A very effective way to field the right team is to start with an early career development program (ECDP) to continuously bring in new recruits who will shape their careers around the values, culture, and purpose of the organization. A strong ECDP not only helps you build a strong workforce for the long term, but it is also a value-add that attracts talent.

Within the ECDP, leaders seek the most talented people and bring them into the fold early in their careers to shape their paths in ways that advance their potential and help the organization. Successful ECDP efforts recruit interns, typically during summer breaks, to work in their areas of interest. We partnered the interns with an engaging leader and provided cohort programs on leadership, communications, and other skills. These sessions helped the interns fine-tune their skills and balance what they may not have learned in formal education.

Interns learned about the company, its culture, and potential career opportunities. The ECDP would direct the interns to put these lessons and experiences together to participate in a team project and report out at the end of their internship on the value of these projects. The internship segment of the ECDP would conclude with an assess-

> *A strong ECDP not only helps you build a strong workforce for the long term, but it is also a value-add that attracts talent.*

ment conference to determine what career path the interns might envision with the company after college and for leadership to determine if specific interns should be offered full-time positions in the rotational program.

Where they show aptitude and potential, interns are brought back as new hires from college; essentially, the high quality candidates are recruited once and hired twice. This builds a sense of continuity and loyalty and establishes that these associates are in a culture where they can experience professional growth.

The rotational program is the real meat of an ECDP. Many college graduates seeking their first position really don't know what they want to do and may not even know what they can do in their careers—they may not even know what is possible. We use the first two years after hiring early career talent to move associates through different roles as close to their stated objectives as possible and at least one role that is outside of their assumed preferences but that leadership believes will benefit the associate.

The rotational program is structured with proactive mentorship, shared peer development, and cultural support. Near the end of the program, leadership collaborates with the stakeholders to determine the first committed role. This approach sets new talent up for success by helping them learn the business from multiple angles while they get exposure, create a cohort of associates for support and networking, and gain the recognition of senior leaders who can sponsor and champion their career growth.

Of course, not every role can be filled from an ECDP, and intermediate and advanced roles will need to be filled. When it comes to your associates and smaller team structures, it's crucial to establish and nurture mutual trust and respect and open two-way communication to build and sustain collaborative growth at every level of the organization. By engaging at all levels, you not only communicate the motivations and goals of the leadership, you begin to understand what motivates each level of the organization.

Recognizing the intrinsic motivations of your associates decomplifies your ability to communicate with and motivate the workforce. Too often, people write off empathy, emotional intelligence, and employee engagement as *nice to have* approaches, and these are the first things to fall by the wayside when times get tough. At worst, treating employees with respect and being accountable to them are seen as touchy-feely nonsense. I argue that it is neither nice to have nor nonsense. Empathy and understanding make the difference between certain failure and limitless potential. If you're not a company people want to work for, the people working for you eventually won't want to be there either, or that disengagement is disastrous to business.

So let's talk about what it takes to be a company people want to work for. People want to work for a great company because they believe in its purpose, and values, which are clearly articulated through its culture. People genuinely want to be engaged and contribute. They believe their contribution is valuable and can make a difference. They also believe they can realize their personal and career aspirations at a great company.

As you are building toward greatness, treating people like they already work for a great company motivates them to contribute to improvement. Employee engagement happens when you harness the innate desire of individuals to contribute and grow with the sustained belief that they can do so under your leadership. That is how you achieve breakthrough results.

As leaders, we communicate the organizational why (our values) that matter and translate the organizational how (our strategy) into relevant, consistent, and meaningful messages for the employees at every level. Every person, at every level of the company, should understand how their daily work matters and contributes to achieving that strategy and how to align with other teams throughout the organization to deliver breakthrough performance. This linkage provides the foundation for engagement.

Engagement matters because companies with an engaged workforce outperform their competitors. Studies show that engaged employees drive higher customer satisfaction, higher earnings, stronger growth, and more innovation. Specifically,

> *Employee engagement directly affects your ability to serve customers, be a place people want to work, and deliver for stakeholders, all of which are necessary to be a great company.*

companies with higher levels of employee engagement experience 23 percent greater profitability and 81 percent lower absenteeism. This translates into 18 percent higher revenue growth and an increase of 18 percent in productivity. A Gallup study found that highly engaged teams were more resilient than their peers during the last two recessions.[8] Most importantly, engaged employees, like Max and Julidar's team in Indonesia, are passionate about their jobs and put discretionary effort into their work.

However, as much as engaged employees drive results, on the other end of the spectrum, actively disengaged employees prevent you from achieving breakthrough performance. One disengaged employee causes a drag on the productivity of those around them, and a disengaged workforce can drag down the company. Therefore, culture and employee engagement matter. Employee satisfaction matters; you cannot win without it.

Employee engagement directly affects your ability to serve customers, be a place people want to work, and deliver for stakeholders, all of which are necessary to be a great company. Leaders affect engagement for everyone in the organization. One disengaged leader is a model for a disengaged workforce. Leaders are responsible for disengaged organizations, and their attention to the issue affects every person at every level. Highly engaged leaders and leaders who create and stimulate highly engaged teams, however, bring an infectious positive energy that affects all levels of an organization. When employee engagement is not a strategy at all levels of the organization and is not modeled by all levels of leadership, associates are likely to see it as a non-priority and disengage. Listening to and understanding

8   James K. Harter, Frank L. Schmidt, Sangeeta Agrawal, Stephanie K. Plowman, and Anthony T. Blue, "Increased Business Value for Positive Job Attitudes during Economic Recessions: A Meta-Analysis and SEM Analysis," *Human Performance* 33(4): 307–30. https://doi.org/10.1080/08959285.2020.1758702.

how disengagement impacts your business provides access to crucial signs and signals from your associates. Conversely, if you ignore those signs and signals, associates will stop sharing them. Feedback loops are essential for healthy communication, so to benefit from them, you need to be demonstratively receptive. Just like strategy and execution, employee engagement requires the same level of alignment across the entire venture.

You might think, "well, this is all easy for you to say, Gary." But I learned these lessons the hard way. I have been guilty of missing the mark with associates by not fully understanding their motivations. In one case, a manager working on my team was doing a decent job, although not knocking it out of the park. While I was not particularly pleased with the rate of growth in their area, they met their objectives.

While I was made aware of some less than stellar relationship issues and management practices on the team, none rose to the level of a major issue on their own nor seemed to affect the ability to get the work done. In retrospect, I may have overlooked these signs because the effort of making a change seemed more painful than living with the occasional comments from members of his team. It finally came to a head, and I decided to replace him.

With new leadership, fresh eyes, and a more decomplified leadership approach, the team excelled and really stood out in delivering for our customers and the company. Yet, that's not the end of the story.

I had the opportunity to see that former manager sometime later. Apparently, he had been volunteering outside of work with a nonprofit organization for quite some time and was passionate about their mission. He admitted to doing the bare minimum at work so he would have time for the volunteer work. He ended up getting a full-time job with the nonprofit and was feeling engaged and fulfilled.

He actually thanked me for firing him and giving him the kick that he needed to go do what he really wanted to.

I was happy he found his calling. I also felt terrible that I never really listened to, and more accurately, never really asked, about his motivations and aspirations. It changed my approach to developmental discussions and toward looking for signs of engagement.

That was not my only mistake in my long career. I also didn't get it right with a high potential, high performing leader on my team who delivered excellent work on everything. This leader was given a lot of important and visible projects. He was the model leader of a high performing team who seemed totally engaged, was on every list in the talent review, and was positioned to move through the ranks.

I was completely shocked, then, when he left. He moved on for a promotion that he could not see coming anytime soon with us. We kept giving him more and more responsibility and more jobs to do, but we didn't promote him properly. To this day, this is one of my most regrettable talent losses. I blame this loss solely on myself for not actively listening, thinking only about the current mission and the challenges of our transformation. I knew this leader was good and would rise in the company. He just didn't see it or hear it enough, so he went elsewhere to get the promotion, and the title he absolutely deserved.

These are examples of what can happen when we do not fully and actively listen and engage in understanding associates' motivations and aspirations. They served as a motivation for me to make sure that I got it right going forward, and they were the very real impetus for developing the ideals shared in this chapter.

Getting it right comes down to asking questions and actively listening to understand aspirations and motivations. Getting it right means understanding strengths and weaknesses and aligning individual and organizational needs and objectives. It means putting people in situations where they can develop, grow, and deliver value for the company while also providing the support necessary to ensure their success.

I can recount numerous examples where matching associates' aspirations and motivations with business needs paid off for both the associate and the business. In almost every case, they brought their strengths to the new assignment, and they brought those all-important fresh eyes. They asked questions, expanded their experience, and often developed new ways to think about a problem, deliver a solution, or grow a business.

One associate was a successful finance leader with a desire for general management whose career was somewhat affected by functional bias. We expanded the role to encompass developmental opportunities that included operational, business development, and commercial responsibilities. Another associate was a strong commercial leader who was also aspiring to general management. We broadened their experiences with operations responsibilities and the leadership of a significant strategic initiative. In both cases, these associates went on to more senior positions and the general management roles they desired.

Full situational placements may be more preferable, though they are not always available. Project and bubble assignments are a good way to develop, broaden, and demonstrate capabilities. Examples of these types of projects and assignments include the development of a significant strategic project, a divestiture or acquisition, securing or improving a commercial opportunity, expanding or even closing an operational facility, to name a few. Supporting and proactively working toward this type of development led to engagement, fulfillment, and meaningful business outcomes for both the associate and the enterprise. Contrast this to the similar personal outcomes of the former associates mentioned earlier who fulfilled their aspirations but without the mutual benefit of the company.

Organizations that drive and sustain strong cultural environments with people who subscribe to the definition of a great company don't experience wide spread disengagement. At great companies or companies that genuinely aspire to greatness, employees want to work there and are, consequently, engaged. Engaged employees feel empowered to contribute to the larger mission and do the right thing. Employee engagement is a spectrum of interest and commitment. Disengagement is at one end of that spectrum, and breakthrough performance is at the opposite end.

If associates put in great effort without understanding the link between their work or contributions and the mission and greater good of the organization, they eventually burn out. Burnout makes it difficult for workers to connect their efforts to what's in it for them in their employment. Sustained employee engagement requires engaged leaders.

Engaged leaders produce engaged employees through example, inspiration, motivation, and guidance. Modeling the desired behavior creates a culture of breakthrough performance.

Engaged leaders produce engaged employees through example, inspiration, motivation, and guidance. Modeling the desired behavior creates a culture of breakthrough performance. Julidar Amiruddin demonstrates the importance leaders play in delivering engaged associates and organizations through her efforts to engage associates every day. Leaders impact more than themselves and their own standard work products. The relationship of leaders with associates is shown in their engagement scores. Those scores and other criteria are an indication of how effective they are at leadership. A leader's influence cannot be underestimated, and a truly engaging leader like Julidar positively impacts all levels of their organization.

It's also the job of leaders to make sure teams know that it's not just what everyone does as an organization that matters, but *how* it is done, both as individuals and as a whole, that makes the biggest difference. Psychologically, employees have always cared about purpose and taking pride in their work, but now leaders can hear it directly from them. Employees are telling anyone who will listen on social media and in private conversations that values matter. They want to feel like they are part of something larger than themselves, and if they don't, they collect a paycheck and will leave when they find something new.

As leaders, I'm sure you've heard the term *quiet quitting*. While this is not a new reality, the openness of discussing it publicly should get our attention. I genuinely believe that everyone wants to be engaged and wants to do a good job. When employees quietly quit, leaders have failed to draw them in, but they stay on the payroll. A quiet quitter has silently resigned their responsibility and interest in going above and beyond. They check out mentally while bringing their bodies to work. Honestly, people have been quietly quitting forever. In the past, the quiet quitters might have been called low performers. Call them quiet quitters or low performers, but they typically do not start out checked out. Rather, leadership is failing to draw them in.

Think about each hour that your associates are disengaged and watching the clock as a drop in the bucket of your larger process debt. Whatever you've been focusing your energy on that is not reenergizing and reengaging your workforce is being undermined by this process debt you're incurring. Your talent pipeline is rusting away because you've not maintained it. It's no different than not fixing a small hole in a leaking ceiling, only to replace the entire roof because of the neglect.

When I think of quiet quitting, it reminds me of an experience I had several years ago when I worked at Trane. A team there didn't feel able or motivated to fix what they knew was wrong until they felt empowered to execute and enjoyed a sense of ownership.

A major component of Trane's residential air conditioners is a coil technology called spine fin, and at the time of this story, we could not produce spine fin fast enough to meet market demand. This bottleneck was significantly impacting the ability to grow and meet the customers' demand, meaning that customers were buying from competitors instead.

When our plant leaders proposed that we purchase additional presses to relieve the bottleneck, senior leadership visited the plant to meet with the people running the spine fin operation. Once there, we learned that the plant only had half of its existing presses running at any given time. Before we bought more presses, we needed to understand why half of what they already had weren't in use at any given time.

It turned out that the presses required maintenance and tuning, and those activities meant that half the machines were routinely offline. We asked the spine fin associates who worked directly with the presses if they thought we could do anything to increase the number of presses running simultaneously and reduce the downtime for tweaking and tuning.

Once someone asked these associates, they were a wellspring of ideas. They knew, intuitively and from thousands of hours of collective experience, how to not only improve the maintenance cycle time but also how to improve machine uptime and availability. They also had ideas to increase the actual throughput for each machine. They knew the machines, the processes, and the environment so well that they were able to produce a variety of innovations that were more effective than buying more presses.

Ultimately, we adopted a thoughtful approach to add some rather inexpensive fixes, significantly less expensive than buying new presses. As a result, the spine fin associates were able to get all of the presses running at the same time and resolve the bottleneck.

All this intellectual capital was working on the plant floor, following the orders that were given, but they were not going above and beyond by sharing their ideas. When asked, some of them openly dismissed the proposed solution of buying new presses. We asked them if they knew about these problems all along, and they did.

I asked them why we were able to just fix it now, and their answer was, "Well, this is the first time anyone has asked." Ironically, as proven by the spine fin example and other business examples throughout time and history, the people doing the work are in the best position to improve the work.

Yes, the spine fin team had been disengaged, but were they quiet quitters, just doing the minimum? If so, why? The truth is, it was never really about the spine fin team, in the same way Max's story was not really about Max. Rather, the story is about complifying the organization so that employees didn't feel safe, free, or encouraged to share their insights to

> *People doing the work are in the best position to improve the work.*

solve the problem. These were seasoned people operating the lines, and each had been with Trane for more than thirty years. This disengagement of experienced workers really underscores the job of leaders. It's not that they didn't want to do a good job, but they didn't feel it was their place to solve the problems in front of them. This was a cultural and communication failure.

The fix for the spine fin presses came from the workers closest to the presses because they were best suited for proposing appropriate solutions. The fix for the cultural breakdown was communication, the empowerment, and support to continuously improve their work. To tap the potential of the workforce, leaders need to ensure that the Maxes of the world, the spine fin teams, and the people in every other operation and function at any company have what they need to do their job safely and effectively. The best way to help your associates is to be clear in your communication and listen to what they need. When you engage your associates to solve problems out of their reach by providing resources, ownership, responsibility, and recognition as individuals you empower them to move to the next level in their growth while benefiting the organization as a whole.

It is a leader's responsibility to ensure that the culture is healthy enough to raise, clarify, and align expectations. This is why owning dependencies and removing barriers that hinder the execution of strategies are essential. Leaders must motivate teams to perform at their peaks, and open and flowing communication and support are just the beginning. Once communication improves and the impediments are cleared to help your associates deliver high performance and excellent results, then you need to maintain it. Talent management is a critical, ongoing responsibility for leaders. Too often, however, leaders default to complified talent management practices laden with process debt. The process debt that accumulates when making strategic placements and securing a strong talent pipeline both give way to reactionary hiring that happens only

> *It is a leader's responsibility to ensure that the culture is healthy enough to raise, clarify, and align expectations.*

when someone leaves the company, taking all their knowledge with them and leaving a huge gap behind them.

I believe in and have practiced taking a different view on talent and believe in a strong talent pipeline. First, I committed to helping make good people better (or great). Second, I dedicated resources to ensure people would be successful in their existing roles and in new roles. So, how do you give them the resources, knowledge, development, and support to ensure their success, even (or especially) in stretch or non-obvious roles? After all, if your teams are set up for success and then succeed, so does the organization. If your team is being developed and can clearly trace their own growth to the alignment to the organizational goals, they will be more engaged in your mutual success.

Unfortunately, over the years, I have seen organizations subscribe to three organizational biases that seemed then and have proven, over time, to be counterproductive to success and damaging to their talent pipeline. The first bias is the preference of outside resources over internal promotions. The second bias is overinvesting in training and coaching resources for *bad actors* who are not a fit for the culture. The third bias, which is adjacent to overinvesting in the problem employee, is waiting too long to remove those poor performers, bad actors, and cultural misfits from the organization.

Companies fall victim to these biases when they fail to maintain their talent pipelines. Many companies use complex and detailed organizational leadership review processes to assess and place associates and develop succession plans for leadership roles. While great companies use these in very thoughtful ways as a road map for determining organizational health and leadership development, they are too often only an annual exercise that is put off until the last minute and not given the attention the process or the associate deserves. This is not only a disservice to the associate and counterproductive to their engagement, but this approach affects the entire organization and is not aligned with strategy.

Furthermore, when looking at their succession plans in these organizational assessments, leaders then place internal candidates in longer *readiness* categories for promotion or succession. This is tightly tied to the external hire bias, where an organization fails to prepare successors for roles and uses external hires as a crutch.

Instead of delaying the development of leaders, I have always asked the question, "What would it take to make this individual internal candidate 'ready now' for their next role?"

This often highlights the perceived gaps in the person's skills or experiences that may be needed to be successful in a new role. I then committed to documenting those gaps and collaborating on a plan for the individual to bridge them, whether through development, training, or *situational placement*.

Situational placement is a career development approach that intentionally places talent into roles that stretch their abilities to foster growth with the organizational support to ensure they have the best chance to be successful.

Ultimately, these efforts were centered on managing and maintaining the talent pipeline as much as they were about making an individual successful. Sometimes, this development and the *who is ready now* conversations led the leadership team to recognize unintentional bias and challenge ourselves to either help talent grow or use the talent pipeline to find the right skill set. Sometimes you really do need an external hire, but if you are not thoughtful about available talent and your needs, you can make those external hiring decisions under pressure, and oftentimes to great disappointment.

Sometimes external resources are necessary to fill skills and expertise gaps to accelerate a strategy that needs specific skills or a developed professional for a particular succession role. No one can *always* have everything and everyone we need in the internal talent pipeline, and you still need to operate the business effectively. As strategies and focus change, so do the people and skill needs. New technical expertise for expanding a product line or skills to advance a growth strategy are valid, and external hires are necessary.

However, a preferential bias for external hires, especially in experienced roles, can alienate the good internal resources you already have and demonstrate a lack of faith in leadership's ability to field the right team through sustained and strategic growth management. If your organization is doing a great job fielding the right team, then you won't need to depend on or reflexively seek external talent. Focus resources on growing the people you already have so you can attract and retain talent from within, contributing to a stable and engaged workforce.

Unfortunately, many leaders wait to hire until they have vacancies. Waiting for mediocre, unhappy, or disengaged people to quit before hiring good people complicates your team. Of course, good people leave for good reasons too, and succession plans are crucial to sustaining business success. In my leadership roles, I was constantly on the lookout, creating relationships, getting to know innovators in the industry and domains of my business, and creating a network of potential talent. These were the people who possessed the head, heart, confidence, and commitment to take action and follow through. This is important legwork to keep that talent pipeline flowing.

Recognize the potential of internal resources and grow them to promote and retain them. When you promote internal hires, it's important to give them the same latitude you would give external hires to fill in any gaps and grow into their role. Expecting someone to do both their old job and their new job to get a promotion or after receiving one sets them up to fail. You wouldn't expect an external hire to continue to work on their previous job after you hired them, so why would you expect your internal resources to keep their old responsibilities when they are taking on new ones?

Another challenge for growing and retaining talent is expecting the internal talent to hold the job before they get the job. Many companies give responsibilities or even titles to internal associates without giving those people the authority or compensation that they need to be successful. Again, this is setting the associate up for failure, not success. Rewarding people for great work with simply more work is not an effective strategy to grow and retain talent or field the right team.

We can also bring prejudice into the bias to external resources. We often know more about an internal candidate because we've seen their strengths and weaknesses in real time and often hold that, even if unconsciously, against them in the selection process. External candidates have the advantage of presenting themselves in the best light, often with industry recommendations and headhunter support with their resumes and presentations during the selection process. Rarely does the hiring team see the external candidate's weaknesses or shortcomings until they have invested in a relationship with the unknown quantity. Less-than-great companies often miss out on the opportunity to select the superior known quantity because of this bias.

One way to manage this bias, learn more about external candidates, and make those hires potentially more successful is to use assessments that get to the core of all candidates' behaviors and leadership styles and align those to the preferred fit.

The needs are best understood by applying the same assessment to the existing leaders in the company to see how they stack up and where everyone needs to grow. As mentioned earlier, I like to use assessment and coaching internally to better develop talent and better understand the culture. Using the same assessment for external prospects allows us to fairly compare internal and use the information to assist in onboarding, support, and development to ensure success.

This assessment method should not be the only determinate for filling roles, but assessing talent proactively provides good data to use in selection, development, and placement. More importantly, after hiring or promoting from within, you can use what you learned to ensure the individual develops in their weak areas from the beginning of taking a new position, not a year into it.

When considering an external hire, also be sure to check their references yourself instead of delegating to those who will not work with the associate. Have the necessary conversations with the given references, and ask those references for additional people who may know the individual. Assessments, reference checks and the interviews themselves provide multiple methods to develop equivalent knowledge about external resources that you have for internal resources so that the comparisons are fair.

Another way to remediate the bias for external candidates is by giving the internal candidates the same advantages. Great companies give internal candidates the same opportunities to shine in the hiring process, let them tell their own story without prejudice or assumptions, and use internal references and

When associates believe that their leaders are invested in their success, associates are more invested in their leaders' and company's success.

mentors to assist them. Their engagement survey scores for their leadership progress, assessments, and performance track record should be evaluated to put them in the best roles for the organization and for themselves. Additionally, leaders should make sure to highlight associates with strong potential to senior leaders and the board of directors. We should put them in important project roles and let them shine so that they are known for their strengths before they sit down for an interview.

When it comes to growing and retaining internal talent, I subscribe to a concept I call *situational placement*, wherein leaders look at internal candidates first for new roles, filling a vacancy, and aligning successions. Rather than looking for a new external candidate, determine how internal talent *can* be successful in their next role. Abandon the dangerous thinking that if an internal resource doesn't have *everything* needed for a role, you disregard them and look outside. With situational placement, you grow your own in-house talent before acquiring external resources.

Leaders want their people to be successful and need to give them the tools to do so. This is done by looking at what they bring to a new role and what strengths already exist in the new team they are joining that may be complementary to the candidate's individual weaknesses or development needs.

The benefits of situational placement include continuous engagement between associates and leadership in focusing on skills, goals, and strategy in their professional growth plans. When associates believe that their leaders are invested in their success, associates are more invested in their leaders' and company's success. Additionally, outside resources need time to acclimate to the culture and operations of the organization as a whole and on their team. They may or may not acclimate and last. However, an internal resource brings a track record of loyalty, dedication, and organizational knowledge that will allow them to be successful with the right support from leadership.

For example, a strong leader could be a general manager, but they lack direct operations leadership experience. However, they are very skilled in the commercial, strategy, and finance domains. The solution is placing them in a role that needs what that candidate offers while the team is stable in operations or has a strong operations leader who can complement and teach the new candidate. Failing to develop the deficiencies in the best and highest potential employees causes impediments to their career growth and limits the resource pool to external candidates who may not be a good cultural fit. We should never hinder internal candidates from succeeding by neglecting this mutually beneficial path to growth.

Of course, not everyone is a great fit with high potential. This leads us to the bias of allocating training and support resources to those who may be delivering but not necessarily in the right way. These are people who *seem* to deliver the results but in a dreadful way that hampers the success of the organization as a whole. These individuals tend to resist collaboration, behave in mean-spirited ways, and are misaligned with the greater organization and culture. Many organizations spend time and resources in a remedial fashion, focused on improving associates who clearly have issues to address. They are solving a problem, but that is only one method to affect the health of the entire culture or company. While focusing on the individual problem may yield short-term results, the long-term impact is less effective than using training as a strategic tool to improve the entire organization.

In short, what they do is entirely for themselves, and they cannot or will not share the values based approach. Too often, leaders misguidedly assume that because an individual is capable of the work, they can be coached or developed in *how* they do the work in a team. The biggest problem about trying to coach the unwilling and, therefore, "uncoachable" isn't just the expense or even the opportunity cost of training the *wrong* associates. Focusing on a problem individual who doesn't want to fix their behavior while underinvesting in high performers sends the message to the high performers who are a good cultural fit that you are not prioritizing their or the organization's success.

We want to avoid overreliance on high performing individuals instead of building those same high value skills and talents across the organization. To keep a high performer pinned in a position unintentionally but effectively creates bottlenecks and imbalances in the organization and contributes to burnout and the loss of your top performers. This lopsidedness is an issue for leadership to address, yet many organizations address it by spending money and effort on catching up on talent gaps rather than strategically preventing them.

While remediation and training may be a good first approach, and a good faith alternative, unfortunately it often leads to the inevitable separation of that associate or leader with voluntary or involuntary termination because they did not improve. Instead, bring these training resources with clear skill and growth goals to develop leaders and teams as a group to see more alignment and drive goodness to greatness. The alternative bias is attempting to move the mediocre or deficient to acceptable or good. Unfortunately, we're more likely to terminate them rather than improve the potential of the whole.

Think about it like training camps and clinics for high performing sports teams. If you want results, you invest in the right team and focus resources to continuously improve. You wouldn't spend your entire development budget on the bench and let your star quarterback sit out training. Reinvesting in your high performers with coaching resources and training opportunities is not done to the exclusion of those with growth potential.

I mentioned early career rotational assignments with the ECDP, but sometimes the need is to cycle a more experienced professional into roles or situations to enhance their skills in preparation for future growth opportunities. When you have a demonstrated or emerging leader with a great attitude, putting them in a role rotation to learn a particular business is a great long-term investment in that individual that will yield lasting benefits for the organization. They will also bring those all-important fresh eyes coupled with institutional knowledge to accelerate continuous improvement.

Decomplify how you attract candidates by using the ECDP and developing and positioning internal candidates to ensure the best alignment. Grow and develop talent as part of positioning them for growth into the roles where you will need them, and focus on making good associates great instead of wasting time or resources trying to make bad associates mediocre. Part of eliminating external hire bias and positioning internal resources for mutual success is the leadership assessment that helps us compare apples to apples and proactively put training and growth at the beginning of a role and set the individual, internal or externally sourced, for success.

We have covered a lot about attracting, developing, placing, and retaining talent and introduced some decomplifying tools and methods. The reality is that no one has unlimited resources to add people and costs to an organization. Therefore, decisions often need to be made. When organizations have headcount reduction events, not knowing or owning their talent pool leads to the same reactionary behavior that underpins the quick-draw bias for external hires. This reactionary response has short-term cost savings accompanied by a long-term toll in increased process debt. Again, the value of maintaining your talent pipeline is essential so you don't cut away the muscle of your business.

Conversely, it is valuable to look at where you have created or lived with process debt in your operations to reduce cycle time or await permanent process solutions. This is where the opportunity to reduce process debt, prior to broad headcount reductions, helps you avoid reactionary mistakes and make strategic choices.

In the interest of owning dependencies and weighing consequences and rewards in decision-making, I favor an ongoing process called Empty Seat (or Vacancy) Kaizen. The idea is that every time there is an opening anywhere in the organization, for any reason, leadership evaluates the role and determines if it is critical to fill or to utilize the position for alignment with the objectives, needs, and strategy at the time. By actively owning the talent pipeline, you can avoid too much process debt and unnecessary overhead. In other words, do not automatically fill every position. Examine the role and its value, look across the organization for other needs, and make an informed and strategic decision about where to best invest the resources for the good of the organization.

This brings us to that final bias: taking too long to remove poor performers, bad actors, or cultural misfits. Similar to overinvesting in remedial training, this bias is based on the belief that every problem can be fixed. However, some people are just a bad fit, and keeping them around drags down the people that surround them. That expression, "A bad apple ruins the bunch," is based on the fact that rotten fruit will spread its disease to the healthy fruit around it. This colloquial wisdom should not be disregarded, and removing the bad apples is best for the health of the entire company. The team's larger value is preserved and promoted by eliminating those who undermine their associates and the success of the company, and I call this equation, *addition by subtraction.*

> *Addition by subtraction improves a team or organization*
> *by removing (subtracting) underperforming or problematic*
> *employees and their negative impact on the overall team's*
> *engagement and performance and making (adding) space*
> *for a more positive and productive work environment.*

The bad apples may not always be obvious. If you have lost them or they were not engaged in the first place, you need to let those resources go so they do not pollute the culture and focus your energy on the people who want to advance the mission and success of the business.

Unfortunately, where these biases exist, they complify by adding, often expensive process debt and are demotivating to the very associates you want to keep engaged. This bias toward inaction tends to take solid performers for granted. We see that they deliver high quality work in the right way and expect them to continue to do so while giving limited attention to those who are failing, often willfully, to do the same.

To reward the best people with more work because their peers are slipping is to send the message that their hard work is not appreciated and to miss seeing the full picture. To protect the talent pipeline, I always restricted my leaders to only one, if any, *people projects* for remediation, with clear standards that needed to be met and a clear deadline for dismissal if they failed to meet those goals. More than one people-problem project is distracting to the leader and takes too much effort and time away from their standard work and developing their good talent. Engaged people in the organization always know who the weak performers are, and they will lose faith in a leadership that fails to remove those problems. Lost faith is a huge hit to engagement.

Remember, good people *want* to work with good people who can and will model and mirror good behavior. Focus on developing people from good to great instead of from bad to mediocre, or your good people will leave.

You can understand that managing your team and decomplifying the talent pipeline are critical to every part of running a great business. Constantly and consistently recruiting, retaining, and growing talent is how you position the right skills in the right place at the right time. As leaders, we can effectively decomplify the communication, complexity, and barriers that cause associates to disengage, which will free people up to deliver on the Decomplified Absolutes. Engaged people are focused and accomplish the work that makes your business a place people want to buy from, invest in, and *the* place people want to work.

Think about decomplifying your associates' experience:

- ❏ *How do you assess the engagement of your associates and the effectiveness of the engagement of your leaders? How do you take action to improve engagement?*

- ❏ *What tools and processes do you use to identify and develop top talent and successors?*

- ❏ *How can you mitigate the biases for external talent, remediation training, and resistance to removing bad actors?*

4. Stop Selling, Start Helping

The company that can simplify the process of achieving the aspirations that its customers are seeking will disrupt its industry and market.

—TONY BODOH

The importance of people and relationships in how to decomplify and build a great company through culture and associates extends to customers as well. Leadership, culture, and employee engagement are all attributes of a company that people want to work for, which creates one of the cornerstones that support a great company. The second cornerstone of becoming a great company is being the first choice that people want to buy from. Great companies are those who deliver a differentiated experience *and* are routinely and relentlessly easy to do business with.

People want to buy from businesses that offer a differentiated and superior customer experience. Decomplifying for your customers by solving problems for and with them leads to meaningful interactions and customer loyalty. A decomplified customer experience, wherein your customers find unique value in the product and services they receive *and* they find it easiest to do business with you, is the sweet spot where a positive relationship and customer loyalty are formed.

These three focus areas of innovation define the decomplified approach to the customer and brand loyalty equation:

- Offer superior product or service innovations that solve real problems and capture opportunities for your customers and for their customers.

- Offer meaningful business process innovations that improve the customer buying experience.

- Eliminate negative industry and market paradigms and take advantage of market inefficiencies that differentiate you from your competitors.

Creating the right product offerings along with ongoing innovation are fundamental to a customer relationship. Many companies end there. Innovations in the customer experience and eliminating marketplace inefficiencies are often harder to accomplish but create as much, in some cases more, value to the relationship and certainly more stickiness. These activities focused on deeper innovation are how a good company becomes and remains a great company. The examples in this chapter highlight *how* you can incorporate these activities into your approach and execution to become a great company that your customers want to buy from, and that begins by forming great relationships.

The seeds of positive relationships are planted when you focus on genuinely solving problems or realizing opportunities for your customers and, subsequently, their customers and stakeholders. I always ask my customers to share their perspective by asking, "What is *your* biggest problem or the biggest opportunity right now?"

I also encouraged everyone to do the same when working with customers. Regardless of whether the customers' biggest problems or opportunities were directly related to our products or service offerings or not, these conversations drove a deeper understanding of the customers' needs and led us to better focus our innovations.

These profoundly insightful conversations led to new opportunities to solve problems that existed beyond the direct value of current offerings. The depth of these conversations and subsequent solutions contributed to building a stickiness in the customer relationship that was hard for others to replicate and delivered intangible relationship value. Most importantly, having these conversations early, often, and above all, sincerely, demonstrates your curiosity, empathy, and follow through on your customer relationships. Not only do these traits make you easier to do business with, but they also help create a differentiated and superior experience that separates you from your competition.

Yes, customers derive value from the products, services, and relationships you offer. But they *remain* your customers when you sustain that value over time. Brand loyalty is built upon the introduction of and sustained attention to the value that makes you different and superior compared to your competitors in your customers' eyes. When you consistently build more value into your products, services, and relationships, you create *stickiness* in those relationships where the customer holds equal or greater value in the ease of working with you and the differentiating value you offer than your products alone. This is how a great company is built on sustained value that is consistently recognized by an engaged and loyal customer base.

In this chapter, we will explore and explain how market leaders have delivered solutions for problems or eliminated friction in each of the innovation areas for customers, building loyalty and differentiating themselves and their customer experience.

The tech industry promotes the idea that the best customer service is self-service. Realistically, if customer service has to get involved, the service has failed somewhere along the value stream. That makes a lot of sense for an online customer experience, but sometimes human interaction is a value, not a hindrance. That all depends on *when* humans enter the value stream, the role they play, *what* value they add, and customer relationships.

People like to feel empowered and in control of their business operations and how they spend their money. When they don't encounter any problems doing business with your company, that is one side of the coin of empowerment. The other side is when you can help them solve their own problems that are not directly related to your products. When you truly understand your customer, you can begin to understand their biggest problems and pain points and contribute to unique and meaningful solutions.

> *Understanding and addressing your customers' problems is the best opportunity to differentiate yourself in the marketplace.*

Understanding and addressing your customers' problems is the best opportunity to differentiate your products and services in the marketplace. You can do this through cutting-edge product improvements, efficiencies, and design. When you innovate and create something new that *also* solves your customers' problems, whether those are common industry problems, unique and seemingly unrelated problems, or unmet or as yet unknown needs, you set yourself apart from the competition. Uniquely and effectively resolving your customers' problems or offering them an extraordinary opportunity to focus their time and resources on their individual success, makes your company the clear choice.

Let's talk about how you can offer superior product or service innovations that improve the customer experience by revisiting the situation Club Car faced. Club Car was impacted by the recession of 2008 because their clients, primarily golf courses, were likewise affected. Golf course memberships and usage were shrinking as individuals reduced their discretionary spending, opting out of membership dues and course access. In addition to the pivot that Club Car made by expanding their product offerings, the business spent time understanding their original core business to find opportunities to help its loyal customers and sustain Club Car's market share through the downturn and when market conditions changed. This investment in understanding their customers and their challenges led to several innovations and new product offerings in the golf space.

Club Car's customer base struggled during the recession because of the reduction in revenue due to reduced member fees, golf rounds played, and food and beverage spending. Yet, the expectations of the customers who remained were still high. It was expensive for golf courses to maintain the standard of grounds and services to which their loyal customers were accustomed. Golf courses are highly labor intensive. Maintaining grounds is expensive, and keeping golf cars off the greens and other restricted areas for maintenance and regrowth was a challenge as fencing, barriers, and signage had to be established and rotated routinely. Cutting back labor to protect margins during the recession was a difficult balance to strike while maintaining the quality of their product, golf course, and experience.

Club Car's response to this customer problem was born in an adverse financial climate to help their customers and led to huge, long-term growth opportunities to differentiate themselves in the marketplace. Marrying global positioning technology (GPS) and drive motor controls, Club Car was able to innovate a new product offering called *Visage*™ that reduced costs and increased revenue for their customers.

Visage used programmable geo-fencing and onboard controls to restrict the range and speed of golf cars based on location to protect golf course areas. This also allowed cars to be controlled remotely, meaning that they could be enabled or disabled from the clubhouse or cart storage barn. Also, key operating data, including battery charge status, maintenance requirements, and other critical data, was collected and transmitted. This eliminated the need for this data and these functions to be done manually, one car at a time. It also allowed clubs to secure cars to prevent cars from unauthorized use and be located if stolen. These controls not only offered their clients significant savings during the difficult financial climate, but the controls also became a product differentiator for their clients, the golf courses themselves.

Onboard touchscreens became an opportunity for golf course guests to order food, products, even lessons and additional tee times, and interact with the club. This provided convenient amenities to the users and added additional revenue to the golf course operators. For avid golfers who no longer needed to wait for customer service agents to provide access, keys, or sales services, those time savings were spent on the links. The golfers were more satisfied, and the golf courses were benefiting from the prestige and ease of using Club Car's products.

The success of Visage really began when Club Car recognized and set out to solve the maintenance and cost problems that their primary customers, golf course operators and owners, faced. The solution came from understanding the problem *and* by understanding that Club Car could also address their customers' secondary need for additional revenue within the same program.

The point-of-sale touch screen device in the golf car offered easily accessible golfer amenities like digital scorecards, entertainment, and course hole maps with real-time distances. With this, Visage provided an interactive and pleasing golfer experience to Club Car's customers.

The stickiness of the relationships Club Car built through Visage was not limited to the golf course operators, as golfers themselves came to find value from these technology offerings.

These additions helped courses reduce unexpected expenses as well. The positive golf car control restricted speed in dangerous areas like hills and curves and provided a direct line of safety communication for weather and life safety events. Those safety improvements, added to the restricted access to off-limits areas, the ability to shut the car off and make it inoperable remotely, and the clear ability to see exactly where each car was at all times, drove down insurance premiums for Club Car's customers. These benefits made the value chain stickier than ever during some of the worst financial times in generations and delivered long-term value.

If you struggle to sell your primary product or service in a downturn, becoming invaluable to your customers by helping them solve their pressing issues or capture their opportunities keeps you at the front of the line for when they are able to buy your products again. You will be the clear choice because, when things got tough, you didn't disappear; instead, you helped and provided solutions to problems with long-term benefits.

Understanding your customers' problems and innovating unique opportunities to solve them is the gold standard of becoming a great company. The concept of

> *Visiting customers and observing their work demonstrates your commitment to genuinely understanding and solving their problems.*

GEMBA—going to where the work is done or value is created—works just as well with customers as it does for internal processes. Visiting customers and observing their work is highly insightful, as are workshops with customers. These activities show both the kinds of problems one can help customers resolve *and* demonstrate the commitment to genuinely understanding and helping those customers.

This was such a driver at JELD-WEN that we built an inspiration center to regularly interact with customers in the project design phase to observe and explore what is possible and jointly solve problems with customers at a stage where it makes a huge difference and builds that stickiness. Along the way, in these customer engagements, new opportunities will emerge that can build strong customer relationships as you learn about their problems and concerns. The ensuing communication with your customers will inform design and innovation opportunities and specification adaptation opportunities. Sustained relationships pull the customer closer to give input on trends, desires, and preferences. By actively working on these engagements early in the design and selection process, you place the marriage of the customer's needs and your ability to deliver them at the front of the process and at the core of your business.

The Visage innovation shows how product and technology innovation is applied to solving problems for customers and helping them realize opportunities. Another way to build customer loyalty and stickiness is to improve the buying process and create a differentiated and superior experience.

Trane's customer service center expanded customer loyalty by addressing the misdirected anger and frustration of their customers to redirect a positive product association. They recognized the depth of the problem and set out to better understand and empathize with customers' emotional states at different times in the product lifecycle. When you observe and learn about the mood and mentality that your customers bring to different transactions on the value stream, you better understand what problems need attention during different interactions.

Trane knew that the service and buying practices for residential HVAC equipment across the entire industry were often difficult or even aggravating. The need to decomplify it was a no-brainer. When you added the stress level of the customer to the already messy service and buying experience, decomplifying the experience would be an act of empathy. Trane had a unique opportunity to join in with and film dealer salespeople as they went into people's homes where these conversations happened, giving an unfiltered view into these interactions.

These residential HVAC systems may be a once-in-a-lifetime purchase, so most customers lack any repetitive knowledge about the process. HVAC systems are also very big purchases for people and typically are done under some duress as their air conditioning or heat is down in their home, invariably when the temperature is extremely hot or extremely cold, and subsequently the families are miserable. Leadership at Trane watched these interactions and clearly saw the distress in the body language, the strained tones, eye contact, and fidgeting. Customers felt a clear lack of power and a need for help, and the customers' distress was clearly apparent. This discomfort was happening in the customers' own homes, where they should have felt the safest and most comfortable, and the empathy stimulated in the leadership team was genuine. This experience of watching their customers solidified their empathy and galvanized the approach that Trane took in all areas of the business.

The customer's initial contact was typically with their dealer or the contractor who installed or last serviced their product. By the time a customer called the customer service department, they may have already been disappointed by the dealer. Typically, numerous calls occurred, perhaps appointments were missed, or the wait was extreme. Regardless of the path, many customers were understandably frustrated by the time they called customer service looking for help.

They were usually upset and seeking resolution while feeling helpless and believing that no one cared about their problem, much less their distress. By the time a customer connected with a customer service agent, the customer was physically uncomfortable, highly stressed, and typically extremely angry.

This is not the ideal way to begin a support call with a new agent. After studying literally thousands of these calls and interactions, Trane came to understand the underlying customer mood. Subsequently, the customer service team developed a new response to incoming calls. The emerging standard work for customer service was centered on showing empathy and understanding the issues or problems, even if the answer or solution was not readily available.

They began each interaction with these direct questions: "Do you have heat or air conditioning right now?" and, "Are you able to stay in your home tonight?" With the first question, the agent cut to the customer's immediate need, and the second question addressed the customer's (and their family's) safety, comfort, and peace of mind. Trane then offered to make a hotel reservation on their behalf. From then on, the conversation was centered on the person calling and helping solve their problems.

Less than ten percent of Trane's customers took advantage of the hotel reservation, but the fact that the option was offered made a huge difference in how customers saw Trane and interacted with the customer service agent. The tenor and the conversation shifted to problem solving and empowering the customer during a crisis that had the customer feeling powerless before the interaction.

While Trane did an excellent job on the front lines of addressing the customers' frustration and service needs by meeting them with compassion and proactive responses, the larger problem of the customer buying experience in the HVAC industry as a whole still needed to be tackled.

Trane's customer service was defusing the emotions of the customer and helping them navigate what seemed to be a flawed customer journey. Unfortunately, the legacy buying process for the industry seemed designed to ensure that the customer was limited in the information they could acquire without physically interacting directly with a dealer. Moreover, dealer communications and scheduling accountability were often unreliable. These industry practices were commonplace, making it difficult to buy from any vendor, and leaving customers to feel powerless at a time when they were highly vulnerable—in urgent need of repair or replacement of an expensive essential product.

While Trane did address frontline issues through the customer support improvements, to stop there would have been to allow the accumulation of significant process debt while ignoring the root issue. The larger problem was the disempowerment of customers during a vulnerable time, and that was industry wide. In this case, the process debt was built on the ease of the status quo. Changing the industry would not be easy, but the opportunity was the exact opposite of process debt. Cleaning up the broken pieces would yield extraordinary efficiencies and drive incredible customer experiences.

Empowering your customer to solve their own problems builds affect and loyalty.

Only by addressing the root cause would the solution really resolve the problem. Customer service eased the heartache, but a full measure of change was required to shift the industry and make a differentiated and superior connection with customers.

Empowering your customer to solve their own problems builds affect and loyalty. Sometimes, customers are best empowered through clear information and streamlined conversion opportunities. Trane built stronger relationships with both the consumer and dealer base by tackling the industry-wide lack of transparency relating to pricing and scheduling such large ticket purchases.

When buying a furnace or air conditioning unit, the three primary customer concerns are: *What do I need? What will it cost? When will someone be here to help me?*

The state of the industry at the time was an illustration of disempowerment for customers. Studies showed that customers usually bought from the first contractor or dealer who actually showed up. It's hard to imagine in a day when there's an app for everything that less than a decade ago these questions were not easily answered without several phone calls and an in-home meeting. Trane jumped on this gap in transparency to build a bridge for customers and service providers that was called TraneGo.

This example shows how Trane tackled and eliminated an industry paradigm in the marketplace. Previously, there was no transparency for customers to determine what they might need, how much it should cost, and how to take action to schedule a reliable appointment window. TraneGo provided online, real-time sizing of equipment based on the customer's actual home data. Then the customer was given a cost range based on good-better-best alternatives and was able to schedule the appointment with immediate confirmation on the day and date they wanted in a ninety-minute window versus the traditional half day.

Industry studies showed that on average, HVAC customers saw only one or two dealers in the process, limiting their choices to those who actually showed up. Giving some power back to the customer shifted the industry in ways that aligned with other changes technology has brought to other large ticket and durable goods purchases.

The TraneGo innovation ensured select partners committed to and delivered on showing up on time and honored their agreed pricing within the estimated range. That's what data showed mattered most to customers, and the partners were graded on their follow-through based on customer feedback. Partner failure to show up as scheduled or live up to the price estimates would lead to elimination from the TraneGo program. The power dynamic now shifted to the customer, who was given the ability to pick from convenient windows of time on the date they wanted the dealer to come. Appointment windows were reduced from the traditional 4+ hours to under ninety minutes, and communications on status were proactive and regular.

Between visiting TraneGo online and seeing a partner dealer, the customer entered the purchase process empowered with a detailed range of product specifications, including cost, customized to the specifications of the customer's home, climate, and budget. This knowledge of what the unit would cost, the power to choose between products, and the immediate access to customer service to schedule a visit at a known time all provided empowerment.

To be sure, channel partners were not overly ecstatic about changing the legacy buying process at first but came to find value for themselves as well. The dealers were saved from delivering the sticker shock of the big-ticket price product. Depersonalizing the cost factor to just a piece of information instead of *a human with their hand out* during a time of vulnerability changed the dynamics of the transaction. Dealers also came to appreciate the quality of the opportunities they were now receiving.

The rollout of this platform led to a doubling of conversions to sales for the dealers who participated in the scheduling program.[9] By eliminating industry paradigms and taking advantage of existing market inefficiencies, TraneGo solved problems for homeowners who needed HVAC service and equipment. Essentially, a complex

---

9   Trane Technologies, "2017 Ingersoll Rand Investor & Analyst Day"

process was made less complicated by removing the process debt of bad decisions and legacy challenges that benefited no one.

Dealers also benefited because eliminating those marketplace paradigms around selection, pricing transparency, and dealer appointment reliability enabled the dealers to provide valuable and empathetic services in a differentiated and superior way. Downstream, dealers now left the customer interaction with more than money; they left with a good reputation and the good will of the customer. This establishes a pipeline for more business through online reviews, referrals, and repeat customers should they wish to add regular maintenance, add AC, or relocate or buy additional property. The potential value for the long-term customer relationship shift is infinite.

The fastest path to differentiating yourself as a company is by decomplifying your customer's life through collaborative problem solving. Solving problems that your customers share with you and helping them solve problems for their own customers through innovation in efficiency and productivity is priceless. The innovation opportunities fall into three categories: the most obvious is new product and service development innovations that solve problems or capture opportunities; process innovations that make you easier to do business with by delivering a frictionless customer experience; and eliminating or taking advantage of industry paradigms or inefficiencies. Even if a solution is not readily available, showing that you understand and care about the customer's immediate issue or opportunity goes a long way toward establishing the preference and stickiness.

Whether you make golf cars, HVAC equipment, shoelaces, or computer software, you can decomplify your business to become a company customers want to buy from. Ask yourself every day how you might offer superior product or service innovations to improve your customers' experience, and then use the tools at your disposal to conduct research and hold meaningful conversations to discover the answer. Ask your customers and channel partners about their most pressing problems or biggest opportunities they are trying to capture.

Examine your business processes in the same light and using the same tools, and then offer meaningful process improvements that make your company easier to buy from and delightful to do business with. As you accomplish these decomplifications for your customers, you will build stickiness in the relationships by creating intangible value that customers prize in your business methods and products.

Through these consistent approaches and actions to decomplify life and business for your customers, you will discover opportunities to eliminate or shift market paradigms that will give you a clear and sustainable advantage over your competitors. This is how you become the company of choice for customers and build your cornerstone of becoming a great company.

Think about decomplifying your customer experience:

❑ *How do you focus your efforts to understand your customers' problems and transform them into opportunities?*

❑ *What does a strong innovation strategy look like for your business (product, service, or buying process experience)? Are you as focused on how your product is delivered as you are on the product itself?*

❑ *What are you doing to demonstrate empathy in your customer engagements?*

❑ *What industry or market paradigms could you eliminate or exploit to differentiate your business for your customers?*

5. Commit to the Critical Few

Strategy is a coordinated and integrated set of five choices: a winning aspiration, where to play, how to win, core capabilities, and management systems.

—A.G. LAFLEY

Great companies excel at continuously outgrowing the competition and sustainably expanding earnings over time and through different business cycles. They also deliver a deeper value that customers, associates, and investors prize. Through innovation, product management, and segmentation, they consistently deliver solutions that customers desire. And great companies have a system that consistently delivers innovation and continuously acts to transform the business to meet changing external and internal dynamics and stay ahead of the competition. This approach ensures continuous revenue and earnings growth.

Competitive separation (or outperforming your competitors) may be defined differently for each business. It may be product or service innovation, a differentiated and superior customer experience, or operational advantages. Understanding what will deliver value for the customer and create the *want-to* implied in the great company definition is vital. Focusing resources to develop and execute around these competitive advantages will separate one business from the next and deliver outsized growth. The definition, commitment, and delivery of this focus are your competitive strategy.

According to Michael Porter, author of *Competitive Strategy*, one of the most widely respected books on strategy, a company creates a sustainable strategy by "deliberately choosing a different set of activities to deliver unique value." Strategy requires making explicit choices, specifically to follow some opportunities and knowingly choose not to pursue others.[10] Then, the business builds its execution around those choices. More pointedly, strategy is an integrated set of choices that uniquely positions the company in its industry to create sustainable advantage and superior value relative to its competitors.

> *When creating a strategy, you must obsess about customers in both sustaining and improving customer engagement while also leveling up your customer relationships.*

This chapter's focus is on *planning* strategy and making those initial choices. The next chapter's focus is on *deploying* strategy using standard work tools to deliver on those choices. First, let's develop a decomplified strategy.

A decomplified strategy boils down exactly what a company needs to do to drive performance while establishing or extending a sustainable competitive advantage. Allocating essential resources for primary operations *and* committing appropriate resources to develop and execute around competitive advantages is the surest path to becoming a great company.

---

10   Michael E. Porter, *Competitive Strategy: Techniques for Analyzing Industries and Competitors* (New York: Free Press. 1980).

Your strategy will encompass all the aspects of a great company—customers, associates, and investors. When creating a strategy, you must obsess about customers in both sustaining and improving customer engagement while *also* leveling up your customer relationships through techniques reviewed earlier in the book. The strategy must also address how an organization will field the right team, both in retaining its best talent and growing its talent base, whether through training, hiring, or acquiring the *right* resources to meet its strategic goals. You ignore these essential elements at your peril, as you must account for and set ownership for individuals, teams, and the organization for the dependencies required for success. Finally, even if the goals are lofty, as they should be, the strategy must work to make those goals achievable by aligning your resources against results you can measure. Along the way, you must deliver to the satisfaction of shareholders, customers, and associates alike.

When it comes to strategy, business leaders commonly overprioritize *what we currently do* instead of *what* we *should do* when setting plans and objectives. This type of focus may deliver performance in the short term. However, being shortsighted potentially risks the longer-term growth and sustainability of the enterprise. Avoiding risk is not a valid way to manage risk; rather, this passive approach promotes incremental change or no change at all.

We are often faced with the dilemma of focusing on either growth or productivity. Many perceive a lean organization as antithetical to an innovative enterprise and are drawn to productivity above innovation because it is lower risk. The answer, of course, is not innovative growth *or* sustained productivity; it is growth *and* sustained productivity!

I am asked about this false dichotomy of either growth or productivity so often that it seems to be more ingrained in organizations and leaders than one would think. Too often, bias for action overcomes the deeper thinking required to make choices that will allow the company to sustainably grow and transform to become or remain the leader.

They believe they have to *do something* without necessarily *doing the right thing*. Even successful organizations can mistake strategy as optimization of the status quo through basic incremental changes and improvements. This *kick-the-can* thinking allows them to delay action and keep multiple options open for as long as possible. You can't shape a rallying cry and a decomplified strategy around a laundry list of things you might try until you finally make up your mind.

Failure to act in a big way means incurring and accumulating process debt as the inevitable changes you're not exploring accelerate in the absence of your response. The longer you delay, the more the process debt accumulates and creates barriers to entry and execution when you finally, if ever, create a balanced strategy.

Accumulating and managing process debt can demoralize associates and shareholders alike. Diverting resources to deal with process debt shortchanges your strategic focus. Those resources better serve your mission when they are aligned with your strategy instead of losing focus on addressing the shortcomings that won't add breakthrough value. It's akin to washing your car when it needs a major overhaul.

True growth and becoming a great company mean aligning organizations, resources, and investments around the few critical strategic decisions that will move the needle to accelerate and separate your performance from the competition. Serious growth comes through significant strategic transformation, and that transformation requires substantive, not incremental, changes.

A strategic transformation is simply a change, and the entire point of having a strategy is to initiate meaningful change that brings you closer to a significant and sustainable competitive advantage. The movement of any objective requires some degree of course modification.

Strategic transformations are meaningful and fundamental changes to aspects of the business that position the company for sustainable growth and success for the foreseeable future. Strategic changes must go beyond the incremental and position a company to compete more effectively or to become more efficient.

There are many reasons a business may consider transformation. More often than not, it is in response to external and internal change. Changes may stem from new technologies or shifts within the market. Similarly, new or consolidated competitors or changes to the dynamics of the market where you play can force changes in the economic landscape, to which you must respond through transformation. These changes may pressure earnings or revenue growth, which can force a responsive transformation.

In great companies, internal transformations result from proactive research and domain knowledge that indicate what may be coming, leading to innovation that solves new problems and unmet needs. These companies mobilize strategic responses and transformation to ensure existing competitive advantages remain sustainable.

Decomplified strategies are not necessarily easy to create, but they must be easy to communicate. Strong strategic plans focus resources to develop and execute around competitive advantages that will separate one business from the next and deliver outsized growth. Ideally, using the strengths in one area will help to successfully propel the transformation in another.

The challenge in planning your strategic transformation is to first identify and operationalize the actions that will deliver growth and meet your margin expansion aspirations. These actions need to be a *few big things*. They need to be meaningful *needle movers* that will attract disproportionate investment and resources. It is imperative to figure out what is important to the company and its customers, and then elevate and prioritize what is *most* important.

Traditionally, businesses employed an annual strategic planning process that collected market, competitive, and performance data. Through analysis and conjecture, they then created the strategic plan. While intended to be the road map for the next three to five-year period, propelling the company into greatness, these plans often were unwieldy and often not executed appropriately. Too often, the focus on developing a reasonable set of financial projections that *make sense* is seen as a substitute for an actual strategic plan. Because these plans are often an outcome of the annual cycle of the operating plan and come with a sense of urgency to complete, they are mistaken for strategy.

A decomplified (simple but not easy) approach to a strategic transformation is to boil down the complicated strategic plan to a heuristic map of where the transformation is heading and where it is not. In this decomplified approach, you identify the current state of the business environment, including the strategic issues facing the business, create a clear statement of the strategy, match those to competitive strategy levers, and select the top tactics and strategic initiatives to be deployed. The strategic initiatives to be deployed are called critical strategic decisions (CSD).

Critical strategic decisions (CSD) are the specific choices and actions that an organization considers to be most important or impactful in shaping its future direction.

The unique characteristic of the CSD process is the focus on execution and use of ingrained problem solving and project management capabilities in the strategic deployment that are often reserved for operational initiatives. Because the execution and project management tools are familiar, their use is somewhat happenstance allowing for a focus on the *what* rather than the *how*. When thinking about how to innovate for your customer, sometimes the problem *is* the opportunity, so solving the problem yields transformation. Focusing on transformative strategy that solves problems for the customer and creates a differentiated and superior experience helps refine an infinite landscape of possibilities to a defined path composed of a limited but critical few.

The critical few are areas that can drive outsized growth and deliver the type of transformation desired over time. According to Richard Koch's seminal work, *The 80/20 Principle,* "The 80/20 Principle is most useful when we can identify all the forces beneath the surface so we can stop the negative influences and give maximum power to the most productive forces." Koch goes on to stress the importance to, "keep the *vital few* in the forefront of your brain. And keep reviewing whether you are spending more time and effort on the vital few rather than the trivial many."[11]

Critical strategic decisions are data driven insights. When using data, it is important to use what is available or attainable easily rather than everything that's possible. While there is always the temptation to gather data to support an opinion, it is best to let the data tell the story. Use caution to not rely only on averages and obvious trends. The problem with trying to use averages to understand trends is that those numbers obscure the details. Rather than getting lost in the data or relying on the law of averages, look at how outliers affect the data. This is a technique called "deaveraging." The average is never really representative of the typical behavior of a population because outliers

---

11   Richard Koch, *The 80/20 Principle, Expanded and Updated: The Secret to Achieving More with Less* (Currency, 1999), 127–128.

skew it. We need additional methods to find the meaning in the data, and that's where deaveraging comes in.

Deaveraging is the recognition that, within large data sets, there may be a set of best answers rather than one that fits all. This approach highlights more opportunities through a better understanding of trends, gaps, and outliers that may point to otherwise missed insights by focusing only on the average.

Understanding the outliers is key to understanding your true average. We look at the full range of the data to find the best answers. The single best answer is not always relevant to the majority, especially if it's going to deliver breakthrough, transformative, and differentiated performance. So often in business, the opportunities for true differentiation show up in the gaps and the outliers.

Opportunities exist in the full range of data. Of course, the problem with gaps and outliers is the small size of the sample sets. However, this is why other methods of verification and corroboration, such as case studies and qualitative research, are necessary.

Making critical strategic decisions means avoiding the risk of detouring to the average or, conversely, falling into analysis paralysis. Instead, you use the tools at your disposal to identify your best bets for strategic transformation and set a defined path. This process does not preclude deep dives on data; rather, it uses trends in addition to the deep dive to make decisions in the moment to initiate and sustain a strategic transformation.

Imagine planning your morning commute. You wouldn't wait until every light was green to leave your garage, but you would also be mindful of the weather report and plan accordingly. Some lesser decisions always need to be made in the moment, but the point of CSDs is to make informed big decisions and move in the right direction ahead of your competitors and market pressures.

The CSD process helps keep the focus on what needs to be accomplished in the near term to get started and in the long term to get big results. Within the CSD framework, assess and determine for your team where to play, how you might win in that environment, and what needs to be done and the resources needed to excel.

The Three Horizons Framework is a decomplified way to ensure that the CSDs are appropriately delivering in the near term and extending performance for the future.[12] The near term (or Horizon One) includes consolidating the competitive advantage, making strategic choices, and selecting capabilities that are incremental in nature to sustain good performance or correct poor performance. The mid-term (or Horizon Two) includes developing the *next competitive advantage,* which could take the form of a product or technology or even unfamiliar business models, while developing new capabilities and competencies. Longer term (or Horizon Three) contains new breakthrough opportunities to reinvent the business for profitable growth and sustained competitive advantage.

Navigating the three horizons is an ongoing cycle, not a sequential activity. Rather, allocate time appropriately to each horizon in planning to focus on immediate and long-term returns. Develop strategies in each horizon based on where the business is now, where it is heading without strategic correction, and where it needs to go with a cyclical rather than a linear strategic approach to planning.

Improving and/or maintaining the operational performance of the business in Horizon One is constant. Now never ends, and Horizon

---

12   Mehrdad Baghai, Stephen Coley, and David White, *The Alchemy of Growth : Practical Insights for Building the Enduring Enterprise* (Cambridge, Massachusetts: Perseus Publishing, 2000).

One is simply where you are in the present, so strategic responses are constant. We are continuously and consistently improving products, services, customer experience, and all value adds in the operation to continue to profitably grow and extract competitive advantage. Within Horizon One maintain and defend the core business, but never really leave Horizon One, as that is where the business operates on a daily basis.

Within Horizon Two is a place of constant approach, where the organization is constantly seeking tactical breakthrough opportunities to change the trajectory of the business. That can be operational, technological, and/or business model breakthroughs. Whatever domain that will create significant new performance and competitive advantage is relevant to Horizon Two. Horizon Two is the domain of exploration and expanding business boundaries. It is never in the past, as the business is in continuous motion, driving breakthrough performance.

Within Horizon Three, you are seeking new strategic opportunities to reinvent the business. These are the bigger bets and disruptive options for future competitive advantage or breakthrough initiatives. Horizon Three requires a different level of thinking and capability. The biggest bets are the disruptive options, and while innovation against customer problems is one method for breakthrough initiatives, it's not the only one. When the opportunity for operational breakthrough strategies is available, those are usually good bets. New technology, new methods for production, or any transformation that will dramatically change the customer experience anywhere in the value stream can be breakthroughs. Though Horizon Three is further out than One and Two, it's a constant focus to remain on target in understanding, responsiveness, and abilities to move to be truly transformative.

We must identify and nurture appropriate opportunities in each horizon, focused on a few critical strategic decisions to disproportionately invest resources, money, and time to position the business for success. For example, a business may need to address operational and product quality concerns that have affected sales growth. This is clearly Horizon One. They may also be looking at developing new technology that will allow them to significantly change their product offering to expand markets served or even create a new, as yet unserved or undefined market. These efforts would fall into Horizons Two and Three strategies. As pointed out previously, operational performance improvements (Horizon One) *and* breakthrough initiatives (Horizon Two and Three) are both necessary components of becoming a great company. The Three Horizon Framework offers a way to manage both current and future opportunities for productivity *and* growth. Critical strategic decisions must encompass both.

Ultimately, CSDs are built upon the well-established methods to win within the environment where your business plays. This includes identifying the structure and sources of opportunities within your enterprise. You need a keen and deep awareness of *how* you can win in that environment and *what* resources you need to secure or develop for a successful transformation. As these are set in motion, the CSD path has three major attributes for success. First, the leadership fully understands

> *CSDs encompass both current and future opportunities for productivity and growth.*

and agrees with the nature of the path. Second, that strategic path is disproportionately resourced to the exclusion of other opportunities and closely followed through execution or deployment. Third, the entire organization is mobilized to execute the plan.

No matter how poorly or well a business is doing, it is crucial to honestly evaluate where an organization currently is, and it is important to continuously evaluate where you may need to transform to stay ahead. We must ensure performance continues unabated while looking for competitive advantages and creating new breakthrough performance opportunities. Strategies need to be in place to sustain *and* aspire through transformation to bring topline growth and margin expansion.

Once you understand where you are and where you need to go, the strategic plan and subsequent execution can come together in a transformation. A successful transformation embodies these steps:

- Define, communicate, and align the team around the aspiration

- Identify where to focus and what to transform

- Deploy people and processes required to deliver results

A great example of critical strategic decisions informing the planning horizons is the former Portable Air Compressor business of Ingersoll Rand, which experienced a full strategic transformation in the early 2000s. Portable was one of Ingersoll Rand's most recognized businesses. Drivers passed Ingersoll Rand portable air compressors at almost every road development project, and they were ubiquitous at nearly every construction site. The portable air compressors powered pneumatic tools, including drills and pavement breakers.

The Portable Air Compressor business was well managed, operationally sound, and delivered strong financial results. Its products were well designed, known for performance and reliability, and it was the market leader in portable air compressors. The market, however, for portable air compressors was slowly declining. Portable compressors are just that: portable. They are trailered behind trucks to job sites to provide power for other tools. A shift in how the work was being done had been underway for quite some time. The rise of compact construction equipment, including excavators, wheeled loaders, and skid steer loaders with multiple attachments, replaced pneumatic tool solutions driven by compressed air. In other words, contractors were choosing to trailer more versatile equipment to the jobsite rather than the seemingly limited portable air compressor. Additionally, the equipment rental channel had been a collection of localized rental houses but was becoming consolidated and controlled by fewer regional and national players. These giant rental companies shifted the buying power to apply pressure on the prices that Portable Air Compressor and its competitors could charge for their products, putting pressure on earnings.

Realizing that change was necessary to grow and reverse the earnings decline, they had to transform the business. In the short term, they needed to defend their core business. They could accomplish this through operational excellence, supply chain optimization, and rationalization of the product line. In doing this, they had to maintain quality to optimize customer needs and deliver a superior and differentiated customer experience while reducing costs. These are clearly Horizon One strategies.

Leadership also took a hard strategic look at the business as a whole. They evaluated not just what was changing in the marketplace that formed their operational responses but also took stock of their competencies, strengths, and competitive advantages they could leverage for expanding and potentially reinventing the business for continued future success. The operational strengths that were *required* to defend the current business would build the foundation for expanding and transforming the business in the future.

Portable's strategic direction would leverage their operations, supply chain, and strong channel position to develop the critical strategic decisions paramount to their transformation. Through this assessment process, the Portable Compressor team identified two other trends that impacted their marketplace. The first was a trend toward round-the-clock construction projects. The second was the electrification of tools and solutions over the traditional pneumatic solutions driven by compressed air. Neither of these trends was huge yet, but the fact that they were perceptible was significant in determining a response.

The team evaluated the market trends and their position to reevalute the product and solution definition at hand. While the company had been primarily about providing portable compressed air to power construction tools, they realized a competency existed in using an engine to drive a power source for application specific construction tools. While in retrospect, it seems fairly logical to add generators and lighting to the product portfolio, the company needed an honest assessment of where they were before they could form a strategy to expand utilizing the current operations and commercial platform.

As the leadership assessed, they realized they had great operations and supply chain assets. They also had a low-cost and high-quality position and had already delivered a differentiated and superior customer experience. By leveraging high value assets along with new products, they optimized around emerging trends. Providing lighting solutions to aid nighttime work emerged as a product extension. Light towers are essentially task specific, portable generators that produce electricity to power a high-powered light for construction sites. As an emerging market for round-the-clock construction grew, this was a great option for diversifying the product offering using the competencies and strengths discovered in the strategic assessment. The light tower could run small tools, but it was primarily targeted at that off-hour work setting.

Once the decision was made to design, manufacture, and distribute a light tower product line, it built on the team's expertise in engine application and mobile packaging from the portable compressor business. With the strategic groundwork done and the assessment of their position secured, they were fairly confident they could expand their reach to design and assemble the light tower product line up. The engine in the light tower would drive a generator instead of a compressor, and the packaging very similar to that for portable compressors would carry the lighting apparatus. Components like the generator and lights, which were not core competences, were sourced through partnerships. Addressing a market trend and customer need allowed Portable to successfully expand the business's boundaries. It also opened up a market for entertainment events and venues seeking light for nighttime operations.

The success of the expansion of the product line offering with light towers gave way to further testing the hypothesis to further expand the product portfolio. A full-scale portable generator product offering became the next aspiration. Portable generators would seemingly leverage the same capabilities and expertise that already exist, including the engine experience and packaging, while addressing the move toward more electrification. One study showed that construction customers who were using portable compressors and portable lighting products were, in high proportion, also using portable generators.

In fact, when asked about what generator brands they used, a significant number of customers said they were using Ingersoll Rand generators. That's notable since, at the time, Ingersoll Rand didn't even make or sell a generator, but customers thought they did. This could be that the portable air compressors were so prevalent and recognizable, and that customers misunderstood what they owned. But it certainly gave the brand *permission* to market these products. If there was ever permission to extend the line, this was it.

Portable now felt confident that they could leverage their commercial reputation and strong sourcing capabilities to move into the generator market, but the speed to gain the new expertise in power generation would take time to gain and deliver a full commercial product line. The belief was that Portable would ultimately design and build the line in its own facilities, leveraging assets and capabilities. They determined that it would require new people and knowledge to develop a portable generator lineup and time to develop a full enough portfolio of solutions to be commercially viable. Portable could jump-start their participation in the market with a strategic partnership that would provide technology and intellectual capital they didn't already have.

After careful consideration, a partner was identified that manufactured a line of portable generators whose brand was unknown in North America. Through a manufacturing and branding agreement, Portable jump-started its portable generator business.

Partnerships allowed them to test the market strategy more quickly, with less overhead risk, and to leverage their strengths and assets. The sourcing and partnership competencies they had been building matched nicely with the recognized channel strengths. A strategic partnership would jump-start the expansion without delaying or overinvesting in a ground up product development.

Recognizing the value of the expanded business boundaries, they changed the name of the business to Portable. This new name effectively communicated the aspiration to grow the business through transformation from a singular product-based business and was a motivating move to unleash future innovations.

The extension of Portable into the light tower and portable generator products expanded the business into new product categories and applications and even extended the market beyond construction and mining into entertainment and events while leveraging the operations, sourcing, and commercial competencies of the business. These are a solid example of Horizon Two growth strategies and represent a significant redefinition of the business from Portable Air Compressor to Portable Power. The success of these expansions, both in execution and financial results, encouraged the business to consider even broader, new opportunities to reinvent the business.

Through this analysis, the Portable Power team determined that there was a high correlation between the Portable Power portfolio and a variety of light and mid-sized construction equipment, including wheel loaders, midi-excavators, and light concrete equipment. Studies verified that, just like the previous portable power expansion, customers positively perceived the Ingersoll Rand brand for these types of products and identified channel dynamics that may be in play should they be offered.

Exploring their markets to better understand their customer base provided a deep knowledge of what products customers typically bought and used when already owning compressors, light towers, and generators. This gave Portable both the ability and the confidence to further expand product offerings by leveraging upon their assets. Opening this path led to a plethora of other light construction equipment offerings.

While light towers and generators are somewhat adjacent, further expansion would require significantly different capabilities and resources. Expanding the product portfolio further would leverage the channel, as the studies showed, as well as the newly developed capability to partner for contract manufacturing for breakthrough transformation.

Building on the contract manufacturing process used to jump start the generator business, the new categories were sourced from carefully selected partners. Partners with best-in-class solutions could be leveraged for their product designs and manufacturing. Leveraging the commercial capabilities and the bundling of full customer solutions was where the value was for the business. The transformation of the Portable Air Compressor business to the Utility Equipment business was meaningful and foundational. It changed the very nature of the business.

The transformation changed the culture of the business and its range of product solutions. It did so because it recognized the competitive advantages and operational capabilities of the business could be leveraged to develop a different growth vector for the business. It is easy to see that bypassing these transformational opportunities in favor of the status quo may have proven shortsighted and detrimental. Portable Power sustained its successful position by effectively understanding the immediate need to improve and defend the core business while exploring, developing, and committing to longer range tactics and strategies that would expand the boundaries of the business and ultimately redefine it. Committing to the critical few strategic decisions created the focus to deliver a successful transformation.

To develop and define CSDs is only part of the strategic transformation. Execution is paramount to setting the competitive advantage in motion. Planning doesn't end with the CSDs.

Critical strategic decisions connect the vision and purpose of a business to the priorities to be deployed. CSDs often anticipate opportunities and prepare to adapt effectively to what might otherwise be a disruptive force for the business.

Strategic transformation requires more than an inspiring definition of a great company and a motivating rallying cry. Transformations are meaningful and fundamental changes to aspects of the business that position the company for sustainable growth and success in the foreseeable future. These changes are beyond incremental, positioning a company to compete more effectively or to become more efficient. And these transformations are something that associates and investors can get behind and believe in.

Once your critical strategic decisions are made, you still need to simplify the message so that everyone in your organization understands where you are headed and how you are going to get there.

People don't rally around concepts like productivity, price realization, or operational excellence. People aren't motivated by *what* we do. They are motivated by *why* we do those things.

Establish your process and cadence for determining the critical few strategic decisions that will drive continued success and breakthrough transformations while ensuring that current operations aren't neglected. Next, build on this work with a process used to operationalize and execute against the critical strategic decisions. This work is the means to establishing a framework and standard work for a process and cadence to ensure focus on delivering tangible and breakthrough results from the development and execution of the critical strategic decisions.

Think about decomplifying your strategic planning:

❑ *How do you balance operational and strategic priorities and focus? Is what you do aligned with what you should be doing?*

❑ *Can you articulate the two or three critical strategic decisions for your business? Have you prioritized them above any other decisions or activities?*

❑ *Have you balanced your resources appropriately across the three strategic horizons? How do you ensure process debt is effectively addressed to allow resources to be appropriately invested in transformation?*

❑ *What external or internal forces may affect your growth or earnings trajectory?*

6.

Reliably Boring,
Relentlessly
Repeatable

Organizations don't execute unless the right
people, individually and collectively, focus
on the right details at the right time.

—RAM CHARAN

S tudies repeatedly show a significant gap between strategy and execution. "Three out of five companies rate their organization as weak on strategy execution."[13] Great companies, by our definition, bridge the gap between the development of their critical strategic decisions and their execution, delivering growth and margin expansion. This is why it's crucial to not merely plan but also put your plans into action and deliver consistent communication and results.

We have discussed the development of critical strategic decisions and the importance of focusing efforts on continuously improving current operations while focusing on opportunities to expand business boundaries and reinvent ourselves to sustain performance with breakthrough initiatives. Great companies engage all stakeholders—customers, associates, and investors—by effectively communicating

---

13   Chamorro-Premuzic, Tomas, and Darko Lovric, "How to Move from Strategy to Execution," *Harvard Business Review* (June 20, 2022), https://hbr.org/2022/06/how-to-move-from-strategy-to-execution.

their strategic vision and by consistently delivering on their promises. They effectively *say what they will do* and *do what they say*.

As shared earlier in the book, associates want to work for a great company where they align with a compelling strategy and purpose that they feel a part of and can see their contributions make a difference. Investors, likewise, are engaged by the clear communication of the strategy and purpose and evidence of the company reliably and repeatedly delivering results. We must clearly demonstrate how achievement of current goals is a step toward achievement of the strategic direction. It is not good enough to have a great strategy, then, without execution.

Successfully executing a strategy requires discipline. It begins, of course, with the selection of and commitment to the critical strategic decisions. Then, aligning the organization with a cause and purpose and setting a direction that will ensure sustainable performance now and into the future. This requires an effective and decomplified process to communicate the CSDs, identify the objectives and milestones that will determine success, deploy appropriate resources, establish performance metrics, and check on progress to ensure results are delivered.

After you develop the strategic direction for the company by committing to the critical breakthrough initiatives to achieve over the next three to five years, you will deploy the CSDs (the strategic plan) and deliver results using a strategy deployment process. Since CSDs span several years, break these large projects and processes down into meaningful chunks that align with the annual planning cadence and commitments. Delivering for today is no less important than staying on course with the strategic vision, so a decomplified method is necessary for developing operating plans to consistently deliver performance and provide the financial resources to invest in CSDs. As the development of CSDs is not static and requires on-going process review, it requires standard work to provide a cadence and structure to the strategy development process.

Strategic execution is crucial because it is *how* to get from the biggest ideas to delivering shareholder value and keeping promises to our customers, associates, and community. Moving forward from the *development* of the strategy, the CSDs, to the *deployment* of the strategies, strategy deployment, requires a system that everyone can understand and get behind. Within this framework, large projects and processes are broken down into manageable and attainable tasks that align directly back to the CSDs. Hoshin Kanri is a lean-oriented planning and implementation tool that businesses use to connect company-wide objectives to the daily work of associates to ensure that everyone is working toward the same goals and objectives.

Hoshin Kanri is a lean-oriented planning and implementation tool that businesses use to connect company-wide objectives to the daily work of associates to ensure that everyone is working toward the same goals and objectives.

The Japanese word *hoshin* means compass or direction. The word *kanri* means management. So, Hoshin Kanri, or Hoshin, has been widely translated to mean strategy or policy deployment. Hoshin is a method for ensuring that a company's strategic goals drive progress and action at every level within the company.

Hoshin Kanri involves setting long-term strategic goals, creating detailed plans to achieve those goals, and then deploying those plans throughout the entire organization (cascading). The process also includes regular reviews and adjustments to ensure that progress is being made and that everyone is aligned and working together to achieve the desired outcomes.

Hoshin is a structured approach that includes several steps, such as identifying strategic goals (CSDs), developing action plans, cascading those plans throughout the organization, and actively monitoring progress. Hoshin involves regular feedback and review processes to ensure that the plans are working and that adjustments can be made as needed.

Using Hoshin eliminates waste and the accumulation of process debt from inconsistent direction and poor communication. Hoshin focuses the organization on what is critical and provides the framework to facilitate the deployment of goals aligned to the enterprise objectives both vertically and horizontally. It provides visibility to track the progress of the CSDs (strategic plan), the attainment of the operating plan, and the visibility to respond to challenges or changes that arise in the execution of any plan.

The Hoshin process begins with the development of the strategic direction and commitment to the critical few decisions. The CSDs are the strategic objectives, sometimes called breakthrough objectives, that will define the direction of the company for the next three to five years. You should commit to three or four breakthrough objectives, and no more, to maintain focus and to not diminish resources.

Because they span a number of years, the strategic objectives are then broken down into shorter-term goals to be delivered in the year. This makes the large goal more manageable and less daunting. These annual goals are then broken down further into actionable initiatives required to achieve the goal.

This step-based decomposition of tasks breaks the broader organizational annual objectives into actionable initiatives that are specific to each team or function. Each initiative is specific in nature, is assigned a measurable target, and is allocated the resources to complete it.

At this point, different teams may have different objectives and initiatives to achieve. This is by design. Each team is responsible for different elements of the initiative. However, as each team meets its goals, they all come together to meet the company's annual goals.

Setting the annual objectives and initiatives is a critical step in the execution of a strategy to make and meet commitments. We align organizations *prior* to the goals' hardening. This alignment happens when everyone has an opportunity to buy in, agree to the goals, and establish unbiased and open ownership. Hoshin prescribes a process called *catchball*, which uses a two-way feedback loop to gain agreement about how objectives will be met.

Catchball is a collaborative decision-making and problem-solving method. It involves the back and forth catching of ideas and feedback between different levels and groups across the organization. The intent is to engage in two-way communication where ideas and feedback are shared freely and decisions and commitments are made transparently through informed consensus building.

In catchball, objectives and aspirations are communicated in one direction while feedback, including the capacity to execute, potential roadblocks, and other realities, are communicated back. Catchball is used both vertically and horizontally to gain consensus and accountability for the goals and ensure that the cascading alignment flows easily in all directions. Through these conversations, hidden dependencies can be discovered, owned, and resolved. Without such communication efforts, the different levels and functions of the organization don't know what they don't know, leaving one part of the organization making potentially false assumptions about the commitment, investment, and support of the other toward delivering what is necessary to be successful. Catchball and open communication mine the value of the collective knowledge of the entire organization and shore up dependencies at all levels.

The process of cascading the annual objectives continues at every level of the organization and through each function. Cascading ensures that everyone in the organization is aligned and committed to the overall attainment of objectives that line up with the company's annual objectives. By the time goals are hardened, by definition and plan, the goal deployment will support the organization's annual plan and long-range strategic objectives.

During my time at the former Road Development business of Ingersoll Rand, we were able to use the cascading power of Hoshin to align every level across the globe. Road Development manufactured asphalt and soil compactors, asphalt pavers, and rough terrain forklifts. The company was going through a major product line upgrade and extension. As part of this transformation, capacity constraints were being challenged, and there was a desire to share new products across the various regions in the world.

In those days, it was not uncommon for businesses to operate under a model where the commercial side of the business, engineering and product development, and operations operated somewhat independently with a loose alignment driven primarily by shared financials. The situation was further fragmented by regional dynamics, and it was clear that objectives could quickly become misaligned. What I learned at Road was the value and the power of aligning all of the functions on a global basis.

The power of global alignment was amplified when applied to strategy development and deployment. The acceleration from using Hoshin to align the organization to take on breakthrough change was amazing. Through Hoshin, the global Road team aligned behind the product and manufacturing transformation and were able to tackle otherwise unsolved problems by acting together to share design resources and leverage more global designs to build the products across multiple facilities. Product development and launch cycle times were reduced, allowing Road to enjoy growth and margin expansion as a result.

The process of identifying and committing to the critical few means that subsequent cascading and active consensus of the strategy deployment process forced prioritization of the critical few, driving siloed teams to focus on the things that mattered toward building a great company. Bringing everyone together with a renewed focus on the customer led to engaging all associates and delivering superior results. It became easy, decomplified, to commit to the product upgrade and expansion strategy and to execute the strategy by adhering to shared objectives when the focus remained on what mattered. Through a disciplined review and countermeasure processes, we reduced development and launch cycle times, leading to quicker-to-market offerings and delivering top line and earnings growth.

Alignment gives your strategy wheels, and clear communication and focus give you the momentum to move forward. You need both to engage in an effective strategic transformation. The strategy development and strategy deployment processes both activate and rely upon all of the elements of leadership and a great company presented in this book.

Several examples of the transformation of the Trane residential business have been shared to demonstrate individual elements of the decomplified approach. While they may seem disparate, they are interrelated and came together through strategy execution. Here's how. When we talked about Trane's aspiration to be the market leader, they aligned the organization through its rallying cry to be the undeniable leader in residential HVAC. To accomplish this, they had to understand and map the interrelationships and dependencies of various parts of the company. Then, they deployed a breakthrough, step-function innovation in the service of customers called TraneGo.

Before TraneGo would be successful, or even possible, Trane had to modify their product portfolio, as described. Operations had to be capable of reliably meeting increased demand. These initiatives were identified, developed, and managed using the strategic development and strategic execution tools described here.

Another alignment that needed to happen was around Trane's pricing practices. When trying to develop TraneGo, it was evident that the pricing practice and process would not support communicating specific prices or aligning service providers. Trane had hundreds, if not thousands, of price lists; it almost seemed like one for every customer. These lists were maintained manually, making it a nightmare to change prices. It is not hard to imagine the process debt built into this complified process. To decomplify for the customer, they had to decomplify pricing with their channel partners first.

With all these prices, the original intent was to meet seemingly varying market needs with what they thought was dynamic pricing. However, because it was updated manually and slowly, it was anything but dynamic. Through the catchball process, it was determined that this pricing issue needed to be resolved before anything else could progress.

Fixing the pricing became a monumental task of analyzing and then setting new pricing tiers, but it was worthwhile. Trane went from thousands of price lists to just six. The alignment went down stream, with discussions with each reseller to explain the new pricing program. This new pricing plan would affect their business, but Trane needed to ensure the effect was good. The trick was that while some product prices might change—some up, some down— the actual price the reseller would pay for the mix of products they typically purchased would be roughly the same. The channel partners' earnings would not decline, but efficiency would improve dramatically. Process debt from an outdated pricing process was eliminated. Alignment on an objective to better serve customers, grow the business, and expand margins led to this process improvement. Alignment assured that everyone in the value stream understood the need and realized a benefit.

The magnitude of the price process changes spanned two plan years. The deployment process kept the progress and all its cascading activities on track. The review cadence ensured that everyone could see how progress was being made and that the program stayed on track. Everyone involved knew how important this was because they saw the direct link from what they were working on to the larger organizational objective.

As you can see from these two examples, establishing alignment throughout the organization, at every level, brings together the entire organization to deliver on the strategic goals. Seamlessly communicating goals and how performance ties directly to the strategic direction is as important with internal stakeholders as it is with investors. However, alignment is only one side of the coin. Measurement and consistent performance are on the other side.

Once the goals are set in motion, visibility must remain a priority. Many organizations identify annual objectives and assign goals, but too often these strategy and goal documents live separately from the day-to-day work of associates. The cascading approach and catchball process in Hoshin address this alignment and accountability challenge.

Strategic deployment and accountability work best when the progress of the initiatives is consistently measured as part of a regular cadence to ensure they stay on track to meet objectives.

A visual performance measurement tool really helps. This is called a tracker or bowler (because it resembles a bowling scorecard) and is created and used by the organization or business, functional teams, and individuals. Actual performance is tracked against the target (goal) at a predetermined interval (usually monthly at the business level). We break down the annual goals into monthly goals and measure, review, and countermeasure against them. Countermeasures are risk aware, informed, and targeted actions made to correct course or additional actions identified to offset the potential miss to deliver the plan.

For each team, a tracker is developed that includes a breakdown of each goal by month for the year, showing the monthly goal and actual performance for that month. The tracker also provides a forecast of future performance expectations, as necessary, to demonstrate the expected glide path for each goal.

As a practice, in addition to the metrics for specific goals related to initiatives, my teams included financial and watch metrics on the tracker as well. Financial metrics are the end goal. These include revenue, profit, margin, and cash. These are the results of actions taken. Watch metrics track important areas of the business that may not be under transformation or directly associated with strategic decisions. However, it is important to measure and manage these functions to ensure the health of the whole. Watch metrics might include things like safety, quality, delivery, productivity, and people-related metrics. We have improvement goals on these, of course, as well.

Keep in mind that what might be a watch metric at the business level may be a primary performance metric for other teams within the organization. When constructed properly, this gives the tracker a complete overview of the business or function and how it is performing against the strategic objectives and current performance metrics. Each metric has a goal and forecast. Actuals are populated and reviewed each month.

Using trackers and the monthly review process helps to align the entire organization on the goals and initiatives and becomes a powerful performance management and evaluation tool. The review process gives an indication of performance against the objectives and allows for course corrections or additional actions if not on track. Careful management of metrics keeps everyone informed and avoids the discovery of a catastrophic failure when it is too late to intercede.

Many organizations struggle with the management of Hoshin because of the many stakeholders involved, and collecting information in a timely manner can be a daunting task. The data used should be readily available, provided by the process owners, and used in the day-to-day operation of the business.

Many organizations use a traffic light pattern (red, yellow, and green) to establish status in their trackers. Red and green indications are pretty straightforward. Red indicates a missed goal, and green indicates a met goal. Yellow is often confusing to people; just think about your reaction to a yellow light while driving. Do you speed up to clear the intersection or slow down and stop?

Countermeasures are specific actions taken to address a problem or risk and are intended to mitigate or eliminate the root cause, if possible, reduce or offset the impact, or eliminate the reoccurrence of the problem in the future.

While I prefer the use of an absolute color, either red or green, the use of yellow may be appropriate in limited situations. If the current goal is met, warranting a green indication, but the team foresees issues that may affect the ability to remain green, yellow is a good indication for caution. Caution promotes a healthy countermeasure discussion to prepare for what needs to be done to offset the potential issue and deliver on commitments. However, things get complified when yellow is used to replace a red or missed goal. I have heard numerous explanations as to why this makes sense, including that the goal was almost achieved, that countermeasures were developed or the miss was offset elsewhere, or that the miss is somehow unique and not to be repeated. Regardless of how it happened or what was learned from it, it's a miss, and we need to countermeasure it to understand why it was missed and to prevent it from happening again. Misses need to be discussed to ensure a transparent evaluation of the possibilities and potential results.

Strategy deployment, the cascading of breakthrough objectives, and the management of performance toward them are how to ensure you meet your current commitments and stay on track to deliver the breakthrough objectives. It is important to use the review process to focus on countermeasures and improve the process.

Real-time indications that give us a heads-up about how things are going or may turn out are far preferable, allowing time to remediate and still deliver. On the manufacturing floor, visual management is used to see if operations are in a normal or abnormal state. I often refer to the standard for visual management as "a one-eyed rider on a galloping horse passing by can tell if things are normal or not." This requires simple and clear visuals that tell the story—green is good, red is not.

We are always seeking instantaneous indications of performance to verify status and make course corrections, as necessary. This is called instrumentation. Think of it like the instrument panel on an airplane; you will know your altitude, speed, and direction, and you can correct course as needed in real time. A report gives data about what happened one hundred miles ago, but that's not prescient enough to correct course in the moment.

Instrumentation provides proactive, real-time data to optimize processes and identify issues as they occur. It is different from reporting, which provides a reflective view of activity over a period of time. Instrumentation shows what is happening, and reporting shows what has happened.

The challenge is to bring instrumentation into functions and processes outside the factory floor. A great example of instrumentation that comes to mind is a distribution center that had a daily management board that included instruments for incoming orders, mix of orders, inventory, freight reservations, picking and packing efficiency, and shipments. Each of these "gauges" had an arrow that could be moved to indicate where they were against the plan or forecast for the period, either as expected, over, or under. This allowed the leadership team and those working in the distribution center to quickly determine how the business was performing and make corrections to improve performance by focusing on areas that were not on target and the impact that would have on the rest of the operation. For example, if incoming orders were running higher than expected, they may need to check product availability to fill orders and make additional reservations for trucks to ship. If the mix of incoming orders were different than planned, there might also be an inventory effect, and the margin may be different than planned. Using instrumentation and visual management brings us a step closer to where the work is done and allows us to look forward to avoid future disappointments rather than looking backwards.

The importance of consistent and clear communications and active monitoring of performance cannot be overstated. This requires a consistent and confident message that will align and excite the organization around the strategic opportunities and a confidence in the ability to deliver results. One clear, consistent message across the stakeholder groups, internal and external, is a decomplified approach that will be more convincing and foster more accountability. Associates want to rally around a compelling mission.

Investors are looking for something to believe in too, and they don't like surprises. Investors seek confidence in a company's ability to consistently deliver growth and profit now and into the future. They are looking for investments that are *reliably boring and relentlessly repeatable.*

Investors get excited by companies that are reliably boring with respect to performance commitments. This is not counterintuitive, because companies that clearly state what they will do and then routinely do it are demonstrating strategic vision, strong communication, and the alignment required to get it done. Performance management and the ability to appraise risk and apply countermeasures appropriately to meet the short-term commitments are crucial because they give investors confidence that no one is asleep at the wheel. This chapter has demonstrated utilizing goal deployment to build this capability, which is only boring from the outside.

Relentlessly repeatable comes from having a plan to sustainably grow and expand margins into the future as a result of the strategic plan you have laid out. Investors are looking for more than just a good idea; they want confidence that the idea will *perform* in the real world. Investors look at the company's and the leadership's track records. A clear explanation of the strategy and how it better positions you over your competitors helps investors gain confidence and choose to invest in and partner with you to build value.

Just as great companies field the right team and communicate with associates to drive engagement, the same applies to investors. Investors are, quite literally, as invested in your success as you are, and appropriate proactive communication builds credibility. Each communication to investors should be related toward achievement of goals, including the strategic goals.

These last two chapters have focused on both developing and deploying strategy and delivering results. It may seem counterintuitive to find strategy toward the end of the book instead of the beginning, but that is by design. Everything in the decomplified approach up to this point establishes the building blocks necessary to shape and sustain a winning strategy.

A winning strategy is a lifecycle of sustainably delivering on the aspiration to become a great company. To outperform for customers, associates, and investors, focus on what needs to happen to deliver in the short term and to reinvent for continuous breakthrough success in the long term. Strategy doesn't happen in a vacuum, and the skills, tools, and attitudes necessary to decomplify the route to greatness form the runway for a successful strategy to take off and deliver. Developing a strategy and executing it to deliver results are key to winning sustainably in the marketplace, attracting the best talent, and delivering for stakeholders. A great strategy includes a strong plan, great communication, a simplified business, and an environment where your best people can work together and deliver results that inspire confidence from investors.

Think about decomplifying your strategic execution:

- ❏ *Can you map your strategic objectives directly to the daily work in your organization? Starting with one CSD, map out direct alignment as far as you can.*

- ❏ *Identify areas in your business where instrumentation would be beneficial to your performance and design a gauge you could deploy.*

- ❏ *Articulate how your strategic decisions deliver value for each of the stakeholder groups—customers, associates, and investors. Is the message the same?*

7. | *Impact Your World*

Your impact on the world happens where your intent intersects with your influence.

—AMANDA ROSE ADAMS

I n your life, there are an infinite number of ways you can impact the world around you to lead, help others, and drive opportunity. You control your own attitudes and behaviors, and in so doing, you can influence the attitudes and behaviors of others. This book offers ways of acting within your spheres of influence to shape the maximum impact and begins by suggesting that you decomplify your leadership approach with standard work focused on the very things that will have the greatest impact.

> *As a leader, the ability to impact the world is literally in your hands and being judicious in how you impact the world aligned with your business strategy will contribute to your great company aspiration.*

Regardless of where you are in your leadership journey, you can use the tools presented in this book to decomplify your approach and deliver outsized performance. Your influence, knowledge, and approach all impact each of your stakeholders in many ways and often in ways you may not have fully considered. The values you subscribe to in your business, how you show up as a teammate and a leader, and the way you communicate all matter. You control more of the drivers of the impacts in your world than you probably realize, even including how you define your world.

The attributes of a great company are one that people want to buy from, work for, and invest in. A great company always does the right thing. Doing the right thing is what makes a great company sustainable in the long run. As a leader, the ability to impact the world is literally in your hands, and being judicious in how you impact the world in alignment with your business strategy will contribute to your great company aspiration.

In recent years, almost nothing has brought as much passion as the focus on corporate sustainability, or environmental social governance (ESG), with heightened awareness and expectations from customers, employees, and investors. In addition to expectations that companies *will* solve problems and deliver results, investors and customers also want to know *how* organizations will deliver and with what impact on the environment, people, and sustained profitability.

> *The attributes of a great company are one that people want to buy from, work for, and invest in.*

Sustainability is not an *extra* aspect of a great company, nor is it a fifth absolute. Rather, sustainability is derived from the strategic application and the impact of following the absolutes on the way to building a great company. Sustainability means being able to meet current needs and objectives and do so over a long period of time by being good stewards of resources and the environment, being ethical and transparent in business dealings, and treating people well. It speaks to what a company believes in and how it does business.

Nadia Reckmann writes that sustainability "plays a crucial role in a company's attractiveness to customers, employees, and investors." She adds that in addition to traditional measures of business success like profitability and growth rate, "customers, employees, and investors judge a company by how its activity impacts the community, economy, environment, and society at large," and they "place a premium on working for, spending money with, and investing in these businesses."[14] This sure sounds like our definition of a great company.

So, it simply makes sense that great companies build deeper relationships with customers by helping them solve *their* own sustainability challenges. Additionally, it makes sense that companies will attract and retain the best people who want to work for a company that shares *their* values. It then makes sense that focusing on sustainability as a fundamental element of the company's strategy will lead to delivering better results for a longer period of time. People already care about these issues and want to do good, so it is necessary to deploy the decomplified approach to providing an engaging, empowered environment to develop and deliver sustainability in every element of the company's strategy and execution.

Just like growth *and* productivity, great leadership is not a choice between sustainability *or* profit; it's driving both sustainability *and* profit. The "or" mindset is often too focused on the cost of compliance, risk management, and reputational protection. The winning strategy is recognizing the opportunities for profitable growth arising from differentiating your company by integrating sustainability into

---

14   Nadia Reckmann, "What Is Corporate Social Responsibility?" Business News Daily, 2023, https://www.businessnewsdaily.com/4679-corporate-social-responsibility.html.

the very essence of what you do. It's crucial to reframe the definition of sustainability as a business model that creates long-term value by taking into consideration how the company operates in environmental, social, and economic environments. These attributes are integrated into the critical few choices that form a winning strategy.

Just like growth and productivity, great leadership is not a choice between sustainability or profit; it's driving both sustainability and profit.

Sustainability results when you obsess about the customer, and in addition to providing innovative products that solve their problems and practicing empathy, you make their safety and wellbeing a priority and consider the environmental impact of delivering solutions. Sustainability also comes when you field the right team by selecting diverse minds and experiences to ensure you're continuously improving the whole of your organization with optimal perspectives and knowledge and treating the associates as you would like to be treated. When we treat ourselves and others with respect, we create an environment where everyone will be fully engaged and confident to bring their entire authentic selves, with all their ideas and abilities, to the workplace.

Sustainability thrives in a company when its people own their dependencies and ensure everyone is treated equitably and ethically throughout the supply and value chains. Finally, genuine sustainability thrives when impeccable standards are held to make your organization a safe and reliable bet based on dependable performance and not beset by questionable practices or uncalculated risk. Results and profitability driven by prioritization and clear communication practices help you avoid process debt, deliver shareholder value, and illicit trust. Clearly, ESG should not be an extra objective you add to your list, rather it *is* a byproduct of doing the right things and doing things right.

Just as keeping your word matters deeply for all functions of an organization, saying what you are going to do and doing it are just as important for sustainability. Clearly outlining where you stand, making commitments to progress, and delivering are key components of sustainability. Making environmental, social, and economic components a part of your critical strategic decisions and execution makes it authentic, actionable, attainable, and absolutely profitable. A sustainable competitive advantage is inherently part of a larger sustainability strategy. ESG should not be an extra thing and should go beyond merely compliance or the minimum legal requirement. ESG should be embedded into the business strategy and operations and align with the values and the focus of the company.

Great companies can only do the right thing when their people are doing the right things. As a leader, you contribute to the greatness of your company by how you *show up* and how you model behavior for your team. How you show up as a teammate and as a leader goes a long way toward creating the great company culture. Remember, great people want to work with other great people. Trust, reliability, and transparency are all factors that you can bring to your work every day to foster strong relationships, improve culture, and grow as a leader. We've outlined how leader standard work decomplifies your approach to focusing on what is important and should be done. Your leader standard work models the behavior for your team about

> *Great companies can only do the right thing when their people are doing the right things.*

what is important. I recommend these five behavior decomplifiers to shape you and your team's performance and optimize your positive impact on others.

The Five Behavior Decomplifiers

Assume Good Intentions

Have a view and speak up

Foster inclusion

Prioritize, to decomplify at every opportunity

Be Curious

First, *assume good intentions.* Meet everyone in your sphere, from frontline associates to directors on the board, colleagues, customers, and suppliers, believing the best in people and trusting that you share good intentions. More often than not, you will be right, which will lead to positive interactions focused on a common objective. People may not share the same approaches or understanding of a situation, but if you share the same positive intentions, you can always work toward amicable and effective solutions. Positivity is neither naivete nor gullibility. Rather, positivity is the conscious choice of empowerment through proactively seeking the best options for your organization and your stakeholders.

Second, *have a view and speak up*, and do not assume that everyone knows the same information. You may all share good intentions, but gaps will exist in understanding and information exchange. What you add may fuel a deeper discussion of an issue, provide alternative perspectives, or strengthen a proposed approach. Take the initiative to speak up and reach a common foundation upon which you can build mutual success.

Third, *foster inclusion.* By including others in your communications and decision-making, you maximize the power and the impact of collaborative problem solving. Diverse opinions and diverse experiences bring more fresh eyes and perspectives to the work you do together. Inclusion drives belonging, engagement, and ownership, which are all essential to effective teamwork.

Fourth, *prioritize*, to decomplify at every opportunity. If everything is important, then nothing is important. Just like the best organizational strategies focus on critical strategic decisions, prioritizing your own choices improves the value of your impact. When your workload, personal finances, charitable giving, interpersonal and work relationships, and your time management in all phases of your life are deliberate and selective, your focus *and* your impact are aligned.

The fifth and final behavior decomplifier is the practice of *curiosity*. Curiosity asks questions and seeks answers. It is an active learning mindset that can help you grow, build stronger relationships, and develop innovative solutions. This is because curiosity often leads you down new paths, bringing more opportunities to wisely predict potential outcomes and act accordingly. This is where you will meet new people, experience new ideas and discover new opportunities.

Modeling the organizational and leadership behaviors of the five behavior decomplifiers underscores the elements presented throughout the book. These behavior decomplifiers embody the very essence of the attributes of a great company and the Four Absolutes. You, as a teammate and a leader, choose to be intentional in the approach you take, creating a decomplified culture through how you do the work as much as *what* work you do. As you learn about others and build relationships, you clear a path to shaping your own career while positively influencing the career paths and opportunities for your associates and peers.

Throughout this book, the focus has been on how to lead an enterprise toward the definition of a great company by decomplifying processes and relationships. Additional focus has been on the importance of attracting, developing, placing, and retaining the right team. The lens has been leadership, but now let's turn that toward individuals, including ourselves. It becomes apparent that you do, in fact, control the majority of the elements that determine the path of your career and own your success.

One of the most common questions associates ask of leaders is how to manage their careers and best position for growth opportunities. It is asked at all levels of the organization, and I am sure it is on your mind, too. My good friend and colleague, David Guernsey, created a model that highlights the elements of successful career development management in a decomplified way and underscores personal control over the elements of your career.

The Guernsey Model is a simple Venn diagram laying out three key elements of career development: capability, sponsorship and opportunity. These three domains overlap, and the intersection of these areas drives your success.

Sphere One: Capabilities. Capabilities are what you are able to do and are often recognized by others. This is a result of your knowledge, skills, and experiences. Capabilities are a result of education and training, the roles you have taken on, things that interest you, and your accomplishments. Your capabilities are often defined by these questions: What am I good at? What do I understand best? What am I curious about? What do I do better than others? What tasks do I prefer to avoid? Capabilities are a result of what you have done and what you continue to do. You are in full control of developing and maintaining your capabilities.

Sphere Two: Sponsorship. Sponsorship represents your relationships with the people who genuinely support your development and advocate for your success. These are the people who provide advice and support, act as a sounding board, provide feedback, and advocate for your success. You can find sponsorship in relationships inside and outside of work. They can include mentors, coaches, colleagues, bosses, and associates. Sponsorship requires cultivation and time and will be built on your track record of success, as well. Not only should you find sponsors for your career, but you should sponsor others as well. You control sponsorship through the choices you make about who to surround yourself with and seek advice from, being selective and giving back to others.

Sphere Three: Opportunity. Opportunity is a reflection of your readiness to take new or next steps in your career. It is based on how you prepare, create, notice, and act upon opportunities and benefits from your planning, hard work, and development of good relationships. To be sure, there are elements of timing and place as well, which is why opportunity is sometimes equated to luck. This just underscores the need for preparation and flexibility. It is determined also by your readiness to leave your current role. Have you delivered what you set out to do, and have you identified and developed a successor? It is not a good idea to focus only on your next role. You have to deliver, and deliver well, in the role you are assigned. You are able to demonstrate readiness when you consistently meet your current objectives and have the support of people around you who advocate for you. However, you do control many of the elements of opportunity and can enhance them by going beyond your assigned work, embracing change, demonstrating transferability of your skills and experiences, and being ready when opportunity presents itself.

Nurturing all three of the spheres of The Guernsey Model gives you the advantage to move your career forward. Seek the place where your skills and qualifications align with the needs of a new role and your aspirations, and be flexible and open to taking a leap that will enhance your capabilities. Under these conditions, your capabilities, your sponsorships, and your opportunities will bring you to the intersection of circumstance and circumspection, opening your path forward.

More than likely, you have been asked to participate in a development dialogue about yourself or with the associates you manage. Development dialogues are usually fairly structured discussions of strengths and weaknesses, desires, and capabilities with the intent to develop a plan to further an associate's ability to take on new and bigger opportunities in the company. The Guernsey Model has proven to be a great guide in preparing for such a discussion and in providing feedback and guidance to others.

The Guernsey Model underscores the control every individual has over much of their own career development and serves to guide your own actions toward success, even as you help others do the same. The Guernsey Model helps develop clear communication specific to career development. Individual and organizational success requires clear and compelling communications, which is another element of influencing attitudes and behaviors to make an impact.

Different constituents often require different things from your communications. Likewise, your motivations will vary by your audience, what messages you need to communicate, and what impact you hope to have. While these messages may be similar and portray the same information, they are variations on a theme. Good leaders are always prepared to control the message and provide each stakeholder with appropriate, clear communications. They are not just reporting the numbers; they are telling the story behind the numbers. They are positioning the organization and the team—where they are, where they are going, and how they're going to get there. The story doesn't change, but for each communication, the message is customized by the effect it is meant to have on each audience.

You should always be prepared to tell the story to gain approval, alignment, and engagement. To do this, your *at-the-ready* presentation types should include the investment pitch, the business or board update, the town hall message, the customer story, and a thought leadership message. Even if you're not in a position to communicate these messages regularly, the act of creating them will elucidate the gaps in your own knowledge and help you communicate key points whenever the opportunity presents itself. It's a lot like practicing in a batting cage so that when you're called to the plate, you have a greater likelihood of hitting a home run.

The investment pitch should be straight to the point to build trust. You want to position your business as worthy of investors' time and resources. For external investors, be able to clearly articulate the trends and opportunities and how you are best positioned to seize them with your plans and your people. When seeking internal investment, be it new equipment, software, an acquisition, or people, you need a pitch. The pitch includes not only the benefits of the request for the organization and how it aligns with the overall strategy and its results, but it also includes the consequences of inaction.

The business update explains the status of what the team or organization is doing, what's going well, what's not going well, what is on the horizon, and the corrective countermeasures in play to correct course and demonstrate what's possible. This is so important because when you understand the cause and effect and can demonstrate you are actively problem-solving in real time, you will build more trust and support for your leadership and those you lead.

The town hall message inspires and motivates associates, communicates the big picture and potential impact you and your associates can and will have. This presentation is important because you have to practice telling a compelling story, building alignment with your associates and peers, and clearly defining the role each and everyone plays. It reinforces culture and values, provides visible leadership, and enhances engagement. The interaction can help you detect gaps and focus on the key messages that are necessary to move the organization toward greatness together.

The customer story explains why customers should care about your products and services and extolls the implications of choosing you over others in emotional terms. Be prepared to share how you are solving customers' problems and delivering a differentiated and superior experience. Remember how solving your customers' problems builds relationships and creates affinity for your brand. Having a clear customer story demonstrates your commitment to both your customer and the business strategy.

Finally, the *thought leadership* message goes beyond your business results and products. This message demonstrates how you differentiate yourself in your business, career, and community. It builds upon your unique capabilities and passions to serve as a launchpad for new opportunities by establishing authority in your industry, product types, processes, or leadership. It is your opportunity to build a brand for your business and for yourself.

Regardless of your present role, you should be aware of your different audiences and their needs to receive clear and effective messages. There is value in preparing your communications kit, honing the details into clear and effective messages, and understanding where you may have gaps in your approach or plans. This highlights the importance of using these communication opportunities to engage in meaningful dialogue that provides feedback and fosters mutual understanding. Thinking about your messaging from various vantage points ensures that you are prepared to deliver the right message to the right people at the right time to make the impact you intend.

Always be intentional about your approach to the impact you have on the world, knowing that each action you take has the potential to make a lasting difference. Your knowledge, influence, and approach will impact all your stakeholders and will be demonstrated through how you perform, how you show up, how you communicate, and what you spend your time pursuing. Your impact will be a result of what you do, what you don't do, and what you allow, as well as what you don't allow.

By doing the right thing and doing what you say you will do—showing up the right way, developing yourself, and supporting the development of others—that impact will be a positive one. The decision is yours on how to handle the levers of impact in your world.

Think about decomplifying your impact:

❑ *How do you integrate ESG into your existing strategy and performance management system?*

❑ *Can you outline your thought leadership message? What would you like to look back on and be proudest of in your career?*

❑ *How do you feel about your sponsorship network? What steps can you take to expand and diversify your sponsor network? How can you be a better sponsor?*

CONCLUSION

It's That Simple

What you do makes a difference and you have to decide what kind of difference you want to make.

—JANE GOODALL

When people make transitions, we celebrate and wish them the best in their next role or chapter of their lives. We recognize their contributions, acknowledge what we have learned from them, applaud the support they have provided, and highlight their uniqueness. Reflecting on individuals whose paths crossed my own, I believe the greatest measure of achievement is the difference each one made during their tenure. The highest compliment anyone can receive is that they made a difference and are leaving the business and the team in a better position than when they arrived.

I have had the privilege to work with some really talented and committed people whom I respect and call good friends. These people have accomplished amazing things in their professional and personal lives and taught me a lot along the way. Long after the battle scars have faded, my typical recollection is of the way we worked together, the seemingly insurmountable problems we managed to solve, and how together , hopefully, we left things better than the way we found them.

Lest I paint too rosy a picture, we *have* experienced and shared any number of unimaginable circumstances where, mostly, people found a way to complify just about anything. We have all experienced, at one time or another, situations that boggle the mind and betray reason. These are the extreme, ironic, and even ridiculous stories that we share to demonstrate just how far off course we can get. Unfortunately, these situations often highlight misalignment with values, including honesty, respect, and ethical behavior.

Countless people over the years have told me I should write a book to capture these stories. One working title for *that* book might have been *You Can't Make This Shit Up.* Chronicling these stories of complification, including the drama and distraction, would probably make for a comical, entertaining, and potentially telling read. To those of you who have been anxiously awaiting *that* book, I apologize. When I sat down to write, it became apparent that the better choice was to try to be helpful and make a difference by offering practical guidance and insights for leaders who want to build strong, ethical cultures where employees and customers thrive.

As we have learned, business is not that complex. There are just too many people out there complifying it. Successful businesses share several similarities and essentially the same strategy. Every successful business seeks to outgrow the competition and continuously improve the business to expand profitability. It really is that simple.

You now have a roadmap focused on actionable steps to decomplify your business and create a culture of success. By emphasizing what *can* be done to create a better business, this book empowers leaders to take concrete steps toward building a great company. And don't we all want to be great? We all want to be the great company that people want to work for, buy from, and invest in, *and* that always does the right thing. This requires building a healthy culture, engaging employees, creating a differentiated and superior customer experience, and delivering sustained results. No doubt you have already thought about how to apply some of the solutions presented in this book to your business.

Leaders must be willing to take action and affect change in their organizations. They must be committed to defining and following their own standard work, which sets the cadence for action using focused deployment of their resources on what matters most. They should routinely go-and-see where the work is done and tangibly understand how value is created for the organization. They must be dedicated to eliminating process debt and avoiding future debts, removing impediments to open communication, and building a culture that promotes the interests of all stakeholders.

Once you've adopted a decomplifying mindset and succeeded in eliminating those complifiers of unchecked processes and associated process debt, it is important to lock it down. Vigilance and constant evaluation of processes and performance will prevent new complification, freeing energy and resources to grow your business and your career.

Throughout this book, I've emphasized the importance of active listening and keen observation. Our entire lives, we have been trained and expected to *answer* questions. For the most part, we have not been taught how to *ask* them. Asking questions is vital to creating a learning organization of problem solvers. It promotes engagement, enhances understanding, and helps teams come to better solutions. Asking questions helps us understand how we can best serve customers and sustainably grow the company.

A decomplified leadership approach makes success easier through alignment. When everyone knows what is important, they can act in concert. How you practice the Four Absolutes (obsess about customers, field the best team, own your dependencies, and deliver results) is visible in everything you do. Through decomplification, we eliminate unnecessary and ineffective processes, lean our operations and functions, and focus energy on the critical few strategic decisions that will sustainably deliver results. Using the decomplifying tools to align strategic objectives with day-to-day execution will deliver outsized performance as everyone has a clear sense of what they do and, crucially, *how* their personal contributions are tied to the overall success of the business. The core functions of your business processes become simple, clean, and uncomplicated.

Beyond the tools and practical tips, I hope you take away a renewed sense of purpose and vision for your organization and for yourself. As a leader, you have a major impact on your team members and the company. Decomplifying begins with you. Understand your motivation, strengths, weaknesses, and aspirations. Decomplify every part of your business, operational and functional, and the processes you deploy. Your every action and interaction provides an opportunity to decomplify and lead your team to focus on what matters most to deliver breakthrough performance. How you spend your time, how you communicate, and how you make strategic decisions will drive your focus to enable greater efficiency, productivity, and sustainable performance.

I know building a great company is not easy—it takes time, effort, and commitment. But I also know that it's worth it. When we create environments where employees feel engaged, customers feel valued, and the bottom line is healthy, we can make a real difference in people's lives. I hope this book has inspired you to take action to create and contribute to a culture that reflects your highest values and aspirations. We can build great companies that make a positive impact on the world. This will be the difference you make.

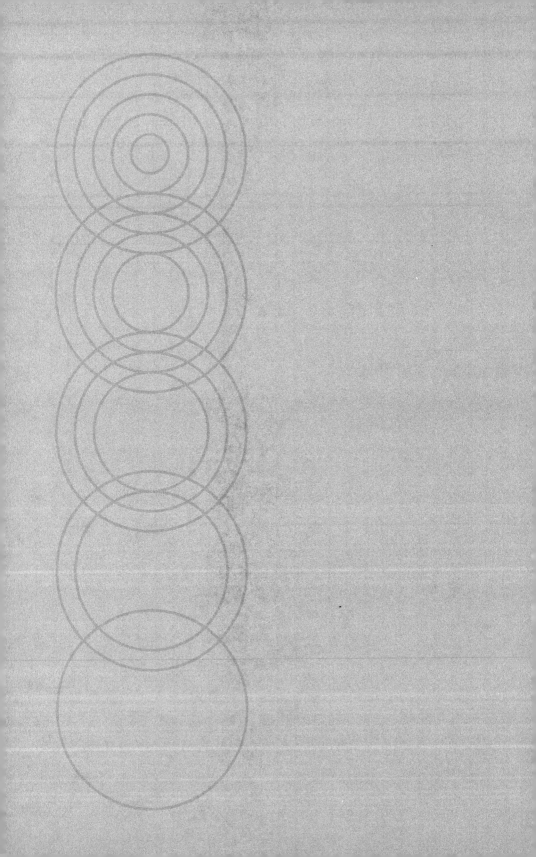

Acknowledgments

When I started writing this book, I sought advice and encouragement from several people who had been through this journey. Two pieces of advice stuck out. I was told that there would be three books to consider: the one you intend to write, the one you actually write, and the one you wish you had written. I also learned that writing a book is a challenging journey and that I wouldn't be successful doing it alone. Nothing could be more true. For this reason, I will take this opportunity to express my gratitude to the many people who have supported me throughout this process.

First and foremost, I would like to thank my wife, Jodi, and our daughters, Allie and Mara, for their unwavering support and encouragement. Their love and belief in me kept me motivated and focused on this project as they have for everything I have ever taken on. Recently, at an event, I was asked what advice I would give my eighteen-year-old self. I said that I would tell the younger me about the amazing woman I would marry who would turn out to always be right. And she really is.

I am grateful to my colleagues and mentors who have shared their expertise and insights with me. Our extensive conversations, searching for answers, have in some way bound us together forever. Your guidance and feedback were instrumental in developing and shaping the ideas in this book. Specifically, David Guernsey, Shawn Laskoski, Tim Craven, Dean Acosta, Terry Dolan, Mark Wagner, Robert McElreath, Doug Wilson, and Mark Stephens for creating the concepts, refining them, and, most importantly, demonstrating them in real life with real results. Ken Martin, Mary Cotler, Alankar Naik, Dan McDonnell, and Gregg Miner: for being my sensei at critical times in my journey and sharing your deep knowledge and commitment.

The best we can ever hope for in our professional career is to have leaders who take an interest in our development, coach us, support us, let us fail, and help us learn. I have been lucky to enjoy this type of sponsorship at numerous points in my career, and the benefits have been long lasting. Thank you to Joe Fumo, Fred Jones, JoAnn Johnson, and Herb Henkel. While each had a unique and effective style, you gave me way more responsibility than I deserved, had my back, and set me up to succeed.

I would like to acknowledge the many associates who have worked with me over the years and taught me invaluable lessons about leadership. Your dedication, hard work, and willingness to go above and beyond inspired me to be a better leader. I am grateful for your contributions and for the trust you placed in me.

Doing anything for the first time is daunting and requires guidance and some trust. Writing a book is no different. I would like to thank the stellar team at Forbes Books who guided me along the way and provided the necessary resources, direction, and patience to see it through. Thank you, Kristen Hackler, Joel Schettler, and Olivia Tanksley, for your professionalism, belief in this project, and invaluable advice.

At the beginning of this project, it took some imagination to take a collection of concepts and stories written by an engineer and craft them into an organized, concise, and readable book. I am forever grateful to Amanda Rose Adams for your partnership, candid feedback, matter-of-fact demeanor, and magician's skill to bring the book I intended to write into the book we actually wrote. Believe me, this book is so much better because of you.

Finally, I would like to thank you for reading this book and am hopeful that you will provide your feedback and your stories of decomplification. They may very well lead to *the book I wish I had written.*

Contact Gary S. Michel

✉ info@garysmichel.com
💻 www.garysmichel.com